T0262457

Torben Betts

The Lunatic Queen

First published in 2005 by Oberon Books Ltd
521 Caledonian Road, London N7 9RH
Tel: 020 7607 3637 / Fax: 020 7607 3629
e-mail: oberon.books@btinternet.com
www.oberonbooks.com

A catalogue record for this book is available from the British Library.

PB ISBN: 978-1-84002-530-9
E ISBN: 978-1-78319-437-7

Cover photograph by Giorgio Gennari; image manipulation by Module Media

eBook conversion by Replika Press PVT Ltd, India.

Visit www.oberonbooks.com to read more about all our books and to buy them. You will also find features, author interviews and news of any author events, and you can sign up for e-newsletters so that you're always first to hear about our new releases.

Characters

ISABELLA
Queen of Castile and Aragon

FERDINAND
King of Castile and Aragon

JUANA
their daughter

LUDO
her bodyguard, a Moor

ANGELINA
her lady-in-waiting, Ludo's sister

PHILIP
a handsome prince

ALFONSO
a spirit

ENRIQUEZ
an artist

ARDILLES
a physician

GRUNT
a murderer, later an entrepreneur

DE LA CRUZ
a gaoler

COLUMBUS
a slave-trader

the last six parts to be played by the same actor
Also: the voices of various louts
and the voice of Thomas Aquinas

5

for
Nigel Barrett

ACT ONE

Scene 1

A room in a royal palace. A cheering crowd outside. FERDINAND, wearing his crown, is whipping his slave. LUDO, standing in a crucifix pose, roars in pain with each blow. He is naked from the waist up. Then, after a while, FERDINAND suddenly stops. He recalls something. He is about to continue. Thinks more. Then he drops the whip.

FERDINAND: Terribly... (*With an extreme effort.*) ...sorry.

LUDO: (*Through clenched teeth.*) I...deserved it.

FERDINAND: You see, I get so full of...

LUDO: It is part of my education.

FERDINAND: ...rage. And then, you understand, I am forced to act out my... How do you mean, you deserved it?

LUDO: By the very fact of my subordinate state. By the very fact of...

FERDINAND: I am a modern man. A sixteenth-century man. A civilised man. I abhor violence.

LUDO: It is acceptable for a master to...

FERDINAND: It is the custom, yes. But I did feel that this time I might have been a touch...severe.

LUDO: Perhaps.

FERDINAND: (*Laughing.*) Erasmus would not approve of this, would he?

LUDO: Erasmus? Well...

FERDINAND: Tell me, what did *you* make of him?

LUDO: He has a certain...kindness about him. He seemed to me to be a...

FERDINAND: You think so?

LUDO: He winked at me when I served him his Cadiz-style sea bream with the Andalusian asparagus and thanked me graciously for his platter of braised giblets even as the gore was...

FERDINAND: He told me, and he does tend to speak with his mouth full, that the institutional function of the church is the propagation of faith and it should *not*, and this he was quite clear about, it should *not* be governed as a state. Calls himself a citizen of the world and says he is not attached to any particular country. If I had the misfortune to originate from Holland then I would probably hold the same view. (*A pause.*) That was a joke.

LUDO: Yes.

FERDINAND: I expect you to laugh at my jokes.

LUDO: Please do not whip me again.

FERDINAND: Then be more attentive.

Loud, aggressive cheers from outside. The gloomy chant of 'Miserere'.

FERDINAND goes to a window.

Seems we didn't quite convert all the Jews!

LUDO: No.

FERDINAND: They found a dozen of these heretics in hiding above a pomegranate merchant's in Toledo.

LUDO: Why didn't they just...leave?

FERDINAND: I don't understand it. They're only words after all. Say you accept the Christian faith or lose a toe or two in the balestilla. Embrace the merciful church of Jesus or be baked alive as midweek entertainment for all these louts out here.

LUDO: The village squares now reek of roasted flesh.

FERDINAND: It's a sickly sweet smell, is it not? Hangs in the air for weeks.

LUDO: Did I overhear your guest say he wanted to witness the horror of the burning today?

FERDINAND: 'The two societies I belong to,' he says, 'are the republic of letters and the Christian church.'

LUDO: You capture his voice and mannerisms well.

FERDINAND: You indulge me.

LUDO: It is a privilege for me to encounter people like this. I am sure that such great men like Erasmus or Christopher Columbus are...

FERDINAND: The man's just a glorified pirate! A syphilitic slave-trader! But... Erasmus: oh, Erasmus...

LUDO: You did seem to be...getting along.

FERDINAND: He opines that the native Americans are actually human beings and, as such, have rights to property and self-government. He seems to think genocide... what was the word he used?...yes, regrettable.

LUDO: It is hard to believe that such a softly-spoken man with such a meek demeanour will be...

FERDINAND: But what you must understand is that the Catholic way of life is simply not open to negotiation.

LUDO: I have never encountered a Dutchman before.

FERDINAND: You have been most fortunate. Now...are you sure you're alright?

LUDO: Through suffering one attains knowledge. So Juana is always telling me.

FERDINAND: But you know, you really mustn't touch my wife. Really you mustn't. It's not right.

LUDO: It was a friendly, comforting embrace. She is an unhappy woman.

FERDINAND: Is she?

LUDO: She cries every day.

FERDINAND: She is the Queen. Of Castile and Aragon et cetera. Why should she cry?

LUDO: For you and for the court, I think, she preserves a countenance of stoicism.

FERDINAND: Of course she is happy. She has everything a woman could want. A fine wardrobe, a whole colony of servants, not to mention an enviable reputation for piety that encompasses the entire civilised world. She, you will recall, is intimate with God.

LUDO: Perhaps you spend too much time hunting.

FERDINAND: She is blessed with every advantage that her rank and her position... How can a man possibly spend too much time hunting?

LUDO: And fornicating.

FERDINAND: Hunting and fucking. This is what I do.

LUDO: It's not my place at all, I know, to...

FERDINAND: You see I really won't have her touched. That woman, though she was forced upon me by my father, is my pride and my joy.

LUDO: Yes.

FERDINAND: Like my best falcon. My best horse.

LUDO: I understand.

FERDINAND: Last week I loaned my favourite mare
to the Duke of Seville and when I saw him canter off
on her, the very thought of his groin rubbing against
her beautiful back, the thought of his sweating gonads
bouncing, though they might be packaged in cloth, the
very idea of them bouncing and flapping and slapping
on her beautiful sinewy back…why it made me…

LUDO: I know you are fond of your animals.

FERDINAND: But I really do insist that my wife, who
is still comely enough, despite her advancing years, to
turn heads and twitch cocks the length and breadth of
Spain, I do insist that… And, for your information, I am
more than simply 'fond' of my animals.

LUDO: She was weeping on my shoulder. It was a private
moment.

FERDINAND: When someone says they are fond of
something one knows that no genuine feeling exists.

LUDO: She says she feels trapped. Emotionally. Alienated
from her true destiny. The affairs of state weigh too
heavily…

FERDINAND: I am 'fond' of my wife, for example.

LUDO: For women, I believe, love is always a high
priority. Even for brutal women of status, sire.

FERDINAND: Use a different word next time. 'Fond'
carries an essence of…I don't know…foolishness.

LUDO: Says she's unfulfilled somehow.

FERDINAND: I…what shall we say…yes, I 'worship'
those creatures.

LUDO: Yes.

FERDINAND: She confides in you, does she?

LUDO: Who else is there for her?

FERDINAND: I don't know...Juana?

LUDO: They are not close.

FERDINAND: She *is* a difficult child. A raging idealist whose face has not cracked into a smile since the late 1480s.

LUDO: A truculent Princess, sire.

FERDINAND: How *did* you learn to speak so well?

LUDO: Juana taught me.

FERDINAND: Did she?

LUDO: She began to teach me Latin when we were children. Taught me the compassionate wisdom of the Bible, educated me from history books. She has taught me to read French, she has taught me Castilian grammar and the catechism. She has educated me about heraldry, philosophy, music and singing. Every day she teaches me the clavichord and the monochord. In short, sire, Juana has transformed a wild savagery into a mild erudition.

FERDINAND: It is, you know, an act of subversion to educate the underclass.

LUDO: She took pity on me. She...

FERDINAND: She is too soft, too sensitive for this brutish world.

More cheers and applause from outside. Hissing and booing, mocking laughter.

But my wife confides in you, does she? Does she really?

LUDO: She confides in me: her whipping boy.

FERDINAND: And by God have I seen her whip you!

LUDO: The mother I never had.

FERDINAND: Even the dogs in the streets have mothers.

LUDO: I was plucked from the shrivelled teat of my own mother when I was scarcely six months old. My sister barely…

FERDINAND: We took you both in.

LUDO: Purchased us.

FERDINAND: Straight off the boat.

LUDO: Straight off the boat.

FERDINAND: It was an exquisitely cloudless day at the harbour. I remember it well. The sun was cruel. The sun was angry.

LUDO: We were alone in the…

FERDINAND: My man chose seventeen savages, all save yourselves now dead, dead from all these relentless floggings I administer. We had lunch in an excellent place. We had grilled sardines accompanied by some strange blood-red fruit from Arabia, and the restaurant had a wonderful view over the Atlantic. Lapping waves. Seagulls.

LUDO: Orphaned.

FERDINAND: And in the afternoon I fucked some skinny peasant girl up against an olive tree.

LUDO: Carried down the plank in a stranger's arms.

FERDINAND: (*Lost in memory.*) She was boss-eyed as I recall. (*Pause.*) They killed your mother, did they? I never knew.

LUDO: Gang-raped her then hacked her into pieces.

FERDINAND: I say.

LUDO: A blade brought down upon her skull, she was cleaved apart right down to her belly. The two sides of her peeled away like broken bark.

FERDINAND: With one blow?

LUDO: With one blow.

FERDINAND: Impressive swordsmanship.

LUDO: You could say that.

FERDINAND: And you could also say that Spain, even a disunited Spain, possesses blacksmiths which are surely the finest to be found on the globe.

LUDO: Apart from Germany.

FERDINAND: There is a case to be made for the Germans, yes.

LUDO: Anyway at the time, I think, I was too upset at the fate of my mother to marvel at the skill of those who were butchering her.

FERDINAND: But you were a baby?

LUDO: I remember it.

FERDINAND: Do babies feel such things? Such gut anger at these little…injustices?

LUDO: Still now and every minute I see those scarred white arses pounding between my mother's legs. I see her face contorted in pain and shame and at one stage, when the fifth or sixth man was entering her, I recall that our eyes met…she was staring at me, she was wide-eyed, open-mouthed, weeping and the look was one of…

FERDINAND: She was a beautiful woman then, was she?

LUDO: And then they sliced her in two.

FERDINAND: Answer my question.

LUDO: A woman does not have to be beautiful in order for her to be raped.

FERDINAND: I cannot imagine ever raping an ugly one.

LUDO: (*Aside.*) And one day and soon I will have my revenge.

FERDINAND: Well, anyway, a bargain you have certainly turned out to be.

LUDO: You honour me, sire.

FERDINAND: Are we not munificent?

LUDO: Taken from the heat and dust and death of Africa…

FERDINAND: You would have been raised amongst barbarians. But now…

LUDO: Bondage.

FERDINAND: Better an enlightened bondage than a barbarous freedom.

LUDO: Of course.

FERDINAND: I own you.

LUDO: But you do me the honour…

FERDINAND: Always do you the honour…

LUDO: Of telling me…

FERDINAND: That you, of all my vassals, are the most beloved.

LUDO: (*Aside.*) I have a lot to be grateful for.

FERDINAND: Yes. As if I had a nigger for a son!

ISABELLA: (*Entering, carrying a framed painting.*) Ferdinand, please...I have asked you, I don't know how many times, not to utilise that ugly, ugly word.

FERDINAND: I didn't know you were unhappy.

ISABELLA: Why should I be unhappy?

FERDINAND: I have no idea.

ISABELLA: I am the Queen. Of Castile and Aragon.

FERDINAND: This is Ludo's hypothesis.

ISABELLA: Of Leon, Sicily, Granada and Toledo...

FERDINAND: Yes, yes.

ISABELLA: Of Valencia, Galiciaj, Majorca, Seville, Sardinia, Cordova, Corsica, Murcia, Jaen, Algarve, Algeciras, Gibraltar, and the Canary Islands.

FERDINAND: I know, I know...

ISABELLA: I am the countess of Barcelona, the lady of Biscay and Molina, the duchess of Athens and Neopatras.

FERDINAND: (*To LUDO.*) Do you ever tire of this?

ISABELLA: I am also the countess of Roussillon and Cerdagne, and the marchioness of Oristano and Gociano. So tell me...what am I supposed to be unhappy about?

LUDO: Your Majesty...

ISABELLA: I am perfectly happy, thank you. Perfectly happy. And I really don't think it falls within the remit of a mere slave, however fond one may be of him, to offer conjectures as to the state of a monarch's spiritual well being.

LUDO: If you would permit me...

ISABELLA: Listen… the time has come for us to say goodbye to our sweet little Juana.

FERDINAND: At last!

More cheering outside. Then the sound of a fire raging. More applause.

ISABELLA: Have you been beating him again?

FERDINAND: Indeed I have.

ISABELLA: You go too far.

FERDINAND: I felt that his head was brushing against your bosom.

ISABELLA: You had no business entering my chamber without knocking.

FERDINAND: I am your husband.

ISABELLA: Not by choice.

FERDINAND: Then who would you have chosen?

ISABELLA: I would have followed my heart.

FERDINAND: God has selected us to rule, to turn the world into a Catholic paradise, not to indulge our oh so tender little emotions.

ISABELLA: Anyway, when you strike a servant, it is intended to be a chastisement, to indicate that some alteration in behaviour is required. It is not designed for a man to wallow in an orgy of violence.

The sound of a half a dozen people screaming. These are the agonised, terrified howls of people being burned alive. The screams continue throughout the scene. The company are unperturbed by this evidently regular occurrence.

Sometimes I feel that all this savagery turns you on.

FERDINAND: I occasionally knock this man about, that is all. Compared with the thousands who have been tortured and toasted at your behest, Ludo's wounds here are as the bite of a mosquito.

ISABELLA: If you spent more time with your family and less time gallivanting with your horses and your...

FERDINAND: Let us not bicker and squabble in front of the nigger.

ISABELLA: I have asked you...

LUDO: After two decades I am becoming used to His Majesty's sense of humour.

ISABELLA: You must learn to respect others, Ferdinand.

A terrible, prolonged scream from outside.

She sets down the painting. It is of a young man.

FERDINAND: He has a somewhat superior air, would you not say?

ISABELLA: He *is* the son of the emperor Maximilian. He has the world at his feet.

FERDINAND: And this is the man for Juana. (*Pause.*) He dresses like a fairy.

ISABELLA: This marriage will benefit Spain both commercially and politically. France will have enemies to the north and to the south.

FERDINAND: But she will have to live in Antwerp!

ISABELLA: We *shall* be pure of religion, race and thought.

FERDINAND: A wet and windy port, full of wool-traders and beer-drinkers!

ISABELLA: She is to marry him immediately and she will be making her home in...yes...Antwerp.

FERDINAND: From the golden sunshine and glorious cities of Spain to the fog and the damp of the Flemish fens.

ISABELLA: It will be a sacrifice that I am sure she will be prepared to make.

FERDINAND: The plague-spreading marshes, the disease-ridden dunes.

ISABELLA: For her country.

FERDINAND: And all that coughing.

A mass is being sung outside.

JUANA: (*Entering, talking at speed as if to block out the world, oblivious to the others.*) Today a great silence reigns on earth, a great silence and a great stillness. A great silence because the King is asleep. The earth trembled and is still because God has fallen asleep in the flesh and he has raised up all who have slept ever since the world began. He has gone to search for Adam…

ISABELLA: I am delighted that you take the words of God so seriously, Juana, but is it absolutely necessary always to speak them aloud?

JUANA: (*Looking up, startled.*) Oh, Mother, Father. Forgive me.

ISABELLA: You are forgiven.

JUANA: Who is this?

ISABELLA: This, Juana, is the man you are going to marry.

A long silence.

He is good-looking, yes?

JUANA: He dresses like a fairy.

FERDINAND: He's from Antwerp.

A long silence.

(*Laughing.*) You will need to wrap up warm, my dear.

A long, protracted cry from outside.

JUANA flinches, her hand over her mouth.

ISABELLA: Why do you still flinch at these sounds, my darling? We are only ridding the world of evil.

JUANA: The screams...they...always...since I was a child...they always...

FERDINAND: Nothing can be achieved in this world without violence, Juana.

JUANA: But Jesus was a man of peace. He...

ISABELLA: Violence in the service of unity and stability is not violence.

JUANA: Then what is it?

ISABELLA and FERDINAND both laugh.

Why are you laughing? Everyone is always laughing!

ISABELLA: You have not heard the saying about the omelette and the eggs?

JUANA: But they are not eggs, Mother! They are human souls!

ISABELLA: These are not human souls, darling. They are Jews.

Another horrendous scream of agony outside.

JUANA: Does a Jew not have a heart? Does the flesh of a Jew not blister and blacken when thrown into the fire?

ISABELLA: The Catholic way of life is simply nonnegotiable, darling.

JUANA: Are not Jews mothers, fathers, daughters, sons?

ISABELLA: Let the Jew who will not convert flee. Let him set up his verminous, heathen heaven in Africa or some treeless Arabian land!

JUANA: But what of the Africans, the Arabs?

ISABELLA: That is not the problem of Spain.

JUANA: But it is the problem of God.

ISABELLA: My dearest Juana, you evidently still do not understand.

JUANA: Understand what?

ISABELLA: You evidently still do not understand what I have been trying to tell you for a very long time now: that God is, and always has been, a Spaniard.

The mass and the screams rise in volume.

All but LUDO leave.

LUDO: So Juana must marry. And therefore my long-awaited revenge. And I feel at peace, yes. This rage... this odious loathing which has been contaminating my blood and fouling my soul since I was a child, shall soon be set free. Shall soon find...expression. And today the poor Queen sobbed on my shoulder. Everywhere in this castle there are these sobbing women, beating their breasts and staring at the sky, imploring the heavens as they rattle and worry their beads and their crosses. But this Queen, even as her ribcage heaved and the tears dripped off her delicate jaw, even as this was happening I could have gladly snapped her pale and fragile neck with my bare hands. This demure little woman, she murdered my mother and yet she thinks me a friend, and oh how she swaggers towards her date with destiny with such conviction, with such faith that God has chosen her. But Spain, know this: there are some who will not remain forever passive. Some of your victims will have no choice but to follow a course of action which is both desperate and merciless. Yes, the day has finally dawned. And the time has come. (*Exits.*)

Scene 2

A bedroom. JUANA is kneeling in prayer. ANGELINA stands behind her. Her bored expression indicates that she has been waiting for some time. When it is clear that JUANA is finishing, her maid plasters on the servile smile.

JUANA: Sex is disgusting.

ANGELINA: (*After a pause.*) Yes.

JUANA: Abhorrent, unnatural.

ANGELINA: Yes.

JUANA: I recently stumbled upon a book of sketches by a doctor from Saragozza and it truly appalled me. A whole page dedicated to that ridiculous, drooping gland and those two ugly, hanging sacks with the unsightly folds and creases. The hairs were like wires, like thin coils of weed and… Ah, the organ repulses me.

ANGELINA: Then try not to think of it, my lady. Try not to…

JUANA: Saint Francesca Romana, whenever her husband came near her, would break out into a cold sweat, vomit blood and then scream for the mercy of the Lord. It is a revolting act that only men, like hogs in dung, seek to indulge in.

ANGELINA: I have vowed that I shall die a virgin.

JUANA: Angelina, I am to be married.

ANGELINA: Yes.

JUANA: You knew?

ANGELINA: We have always known.

JUANA: Yes, but I do not at this moment feel...prepared.

ANGELINA: I am certain that...

JUANA: For this most unwelcome invasion of my tender body.

ANGELINA: He is very good-looking. I have seen pictures. He looks a little like...

JUANA: I do not care for men.

ANGELINA: No.

JUANA: I care for God, Jesus and the life hereafter.

JUANA raises her arms and ANGELINA removes her clothes. JUANA has a huge amount of crucifixes around her neck.

ANGELINA helps her into a night-dress. Slow church bells sound.

How do they expect me ever to sleep when there are always these infernal bells?

ANGELINA: I saw the entertainment today.

JUANA: How was it?

ANGELINA: People were crawling over each other to get to the front. To see the pain on the faces of the...

JUANA: I have managed to go my whole life without ever seeing a burning.

ANGELINA: The thought of burning alive... I have nightmares, I...

JUANA: I also.

ANGELINA: Who dreams up these...

JUANA: I cannot imagine being so brutal. The imagination must be so...twisted. (*Pause.*) They do not burn people in Antwerp.

ANGELINA: No?

JUANA: They hang and they dismember and they disembowel but I am told that they do not burn.

ANGELINA: Am I...to come with you, my lady, to Antwerp?

JUANA: My life in Spain is now at an end.

ANGELINA: And mine also it seems. Would there be...

JUANA: You may go now.

ANGELINA: My lady.

JUANA: And thank you. Thank you for being my friend, my constant companion.

ANGELINA: I am happy to be the...

JUANA: It is strange that my two greatest friends in this life are my servants. And both of you mere Moors. How I would survive without you and Ludo... I cannot bear to think about it. One of you makes my bed, dresses me, prepares my food, the other guards my person every moment of the day, keeps the filthy rabble off me when they get too close. Angelina, why do you no longer speak with him?

ANGELINA: It is him who refuses to acknowledge me.

JUANA: I've seen the way he looks at you of late. Sideways. With contempt.

ANGELINA: He thinks I am now more Christian than Muslim, more Spaniard than Moor. And I've seen the way he looks at you.

JUANA: And how does he look at me?

ANGELINA: He is full of a secret hatred which he hides
from you and your parents.

JUANA: Nonsense.

ANGELINA: And he sees me as a traitor to our people.

JUANA: Nonsense, nonsense!

ANGELINA: Thinks I too easily accept my chains. That I
have become comfortable in them.

JUANA: This is ridiculous. I might own you but I treat you
well, do I not?

ANGELINA: And that therefore my whole existence is
an affront to the memory of those whom Spain has
slaughtered. You must be careful.

JUANA: Careful? Of Ludo? Are you jealous of him? Is that
it? You are in competition with him as to which of you is
my favourite?

ANGELINA: Not at all.

JUANA: Or…do you perhaps…desire him?

ANGELINA: He is my brother, my lady!!

JUANA: I know he is. But I did read recently that you
people sometimes indulge in…

ANGELINA: Ah, the thought of it!

ANGELINA, head bowed, falls silent.

JUANA: Please, I'm sorry. That was thoughtless,
insensitive. Please…forgive me!

ANGELINA: I have the same attitude to all…that as you
have, my lady. But to think…with my own flesh and

blood!

JUANA: I beg you to forgive me. I didn't mean to upset you, believe me! Say you forgive me.

ANGELINA: I...forgive you.

JUANA: Thank you. Now go.

ANGELINA leaves.

JUANA watches her.

That girl has a wonderful, wonderful arse. Yes, I have always been rather envious of her perfectly symmetrical and compact behind.

Laughter from above.

JUANA looks up.

Oh, do go away!

ALFONSO, nailed to a cross and wearing a crown of thorns, appears above. He continues to laugh.

Why are you laughing at me? Why are you always laughing?

He continues to laugh.

Say!

He stops laughing. Is about to say something. Then he breaks out into laughter once more.

Not funny! Absolutely not, not funny!

ALFONSO: (*Mimicking.*) 'I do not feel...prepared.'

JUANA: Sorry?

ALFONSO: 'For this most unwelcome invasion of my tender body.'

JUANA: Stop this laughing! I command you, as a Princess

26

of Spain, to desist immediately.

ALFONSO: It really is piss, is that.

JUANA: It is not...piss.

ALFONSO: Liar, you!!

JUANA: Not lying!

ALFONSO: Dissembler, you!

JUANA: Not lying, not lying!

ALFONSO: Your virginity hangs upon you like a disease. How you pine for a release from it! You lie there every night, alone in that pit, the sheets becoming soggy with salty sweat, you lie on your back, squirming, writhing, your slender fingers...

JUANA: Not listening, not listening...

ALFONSO: You have never played the clavichord with such passion.

JUANA: Oh, rot in hell!

ALFONSO: Ah, your mouth now transforms into that familiar snarl.

JUANA: Go away!

ALFONSO: But oh how the future of Spain depends upon that membrane between your legs remaining...

JUANA: Enough!

ALFONSO: ...unruptured.

JUANA: You are ...crude.

ALFONSO: Always crude.

JUANA: And so what if I do long to be fucked!

ALFONSO: So what indeed!

JUANA: I do, I want it!

ALFONSO: Oh, I know.

JUANA: I have even straddled you in my dreams.

ALFONSO: (*Laughing.*) Oh, I know, I know...

JUANA: Ridden you in my dreams.

ALFONSO: And that most expertly.

JUANA: My nails scraping your emaciated chest.

ALFONSO: Your talons.

JUANA: My fingers thrust deep in your mouth!

ALFONSO: Well, it seems your itch is finally to be scratched.

JUANA: I wish you'd go.

ALFONSO: 'I have managed to go my whole life without ever seeing a burning.'

JUANA: And I do not speak like that!

ALFONSO: But you have peeped from behind curtains, you have been out in the night and examined charred corpses. And how you speak up for the Jews!

JUANA: Listen, nobody much cares for the Jews, do they, but I don't see why they should have to die simply for being as they are. Oh, stop laughing! You think I'm naïve! Unworldly! You think I know nothing! Well, I do know! I do know! You think I only live through my books! That I experience the world second-hand! Well, tell me, what is so wrong with that! Stop laughing! I am not just a figure of fun! I can sit happily in my own room, with a book! That is all! That is my strength!

ALFONSO: You are not happy!

JUANA: I *am* happy!

ALFONSO: Your misery is boundless!

JUANA: Nonsense!

ALFONSO: You long to be probed by male flesh. To cup a man's buttocks in your palms and impale yourself upon him.

JUANA: Oh, please!

ALFONSO: You'd exchange a lifetime's learning for one night in a brothel!

JUANA: Oh, go away! Go away! Go away!

ALFONSO laughs.

Ludo! Ludo!

ALFONSO fades from view.

Ludo! Ludo! Quickly!

LUDO rushes on, sword drawn.

He was here again!

LUDO: The Devil?

JUANA: Yes, yes! He visits me every day now, every night!

LUDO: My lady, I think you…

JUANA: Hold me, Ludo! Hold me!

LUDO: I do not think it wise.

JUANA: Hold me, God damn you, you are my only friend! So…hold me!

LUDO: Your father caught me comforting your mother this afternoon. She was sobbing her sadnesses into my neck. His whip removed so much flesh from my back…

JUANA: I need to rub my despair against the chest of a man.

LUDO: Listen…

JUANA: I beg you, Ludo, as my loyal and trusted friend, to offer me your strength and compassion at this time.

LUDO: My lady…

He goes to her and holds her.

She grabs him hard.

He winces with the pain.

She sobs.

(*Aside.*) Although she represents all in the world that I despise I cannot deny that at this moment, as I hold her trembling body in my arms, that I do feel a slight emotion.

JUANA: Thank you, Ludo, thank you.

LUDO: (*Aside.*) It stirs briefly and then subsides. Yes. The hatred now returns and I am calm again. (*Inhales.*) She has always washed her hair in lavender and this smell for some reason intoxicates me.

JUANA: (*Squeezing him.*) I'm so sorry for this pathetic display, this unworthy exhibition of childish emotion.

LUDO: (*Aside.*) But my people must be avenged and my destiny is fixed.

JUANA: (*Suddenly recovered.*) Tell me…why am I always crying? And why does everyone continually laugh at me for doing so?

LUDO: Perhaps you have yet to cultivate the armour of moral indifference without which it is impossible for human creatures to pass happily through this world.

ALFONSO laughs off.

JUANA: Stop laughing!

LUDO: I was not laughing, my lady.

JUANA: Not you. Alfonso.

LUDO: This is…the Devil again?

JUANA: Always laughing, always laughing…

LUDO: You need to rest, my lady. You have an ordeal
ahead of you.

JUANA: An ordeal?

LUDO: Is not marriage an ordeal for everyone?

JUANA: I will love him, I know. I was born to…love.

LUDO: Though he dresses like a fairy, the man certainly
has good bone structure.

JUANA: I could love a good bone structure.

LUDO: It may well be all you have to hold onto, my lady.

Scene 3

*PHILIP stands alone. He is dressed flamboyantly and in marked
contrast to the Spaniards. He is in a state of wild excitement. PHILIP
is large, well-fed and rather effeminate.*

PHILIP: Three hundred steamed roosters stuffed with
cloves and cinnamon and two hundred wild boars'
heads…I want the tusks still intact, I want them in the
colours of the Belgian flag! And I wish to wash all the
nosh down with ale!

LOUTS: (*Off.*) With ale!!

PHILIP: I desire haunches of venison…I desire goose
giblets, I want stuffed sparrows and woodcocks, I want

rabbits but I want them well-rinsed, rinse them well with vinegar and cook them in their own blood. And I wish to wash all the nosh down with ale!

LOUTS: (*Off.*) With ale!!

PHILIP: Set this all down, people. Set this all down! I want this wedding feast to be remembered. I want it to echo down the vaults of eternity as the best binge to ever bloat a human belly. And I wish to wash all the nosh down with ale!

LOUTS: (*Off.*) With ale!!

PHILIP: I want red deer prepared in the German fashion: baste those dangling carcasses every day for months, inside and out, with wine. Wine from the Rhine, people. Wine from the Rhine. A geezer of saliva erupts from my gob! I want carp and pike roasted in their own silver scales and then I want the fuckers all boiled up in ale!

LOUTS: (*Off.*) In ale!!

PHILIP: I want pear tart, plum tart, cherry tart, apple tart, almond tart, liver tart, egg tart, herb tart, quince tart, mince tart, white tart – watch the heart, don't start! I want apple puffs, snow balls, rice buns, yum yums. I wish to wash all the nosh down with ale!

LOUTS: (*Off.*) With ale!!

PHILIP: So let us call in the monks and then sample the beers! Because it is I, it is I who am finally to be the centre of the whole world's attention!

ISABELLA: (*Entering, wrapped up.*) I always thought that particular honour belonged to the bride. Tell me, Fatty, where might I find Philip the Fair?

PHILIP: Who deigns to enquire after a member of the...?

ISABELLA: The Queen of Castile and Aragon. Of Leon,

Sicily, Granada, Toledo…

PHILIP: (*Looking round.*) Who granted this baglady access to me!!??

ISABELLA: Of Valencia, Galiciaj, Majorca, Seville, Sardinia, Cordova, Corsica, Murcia…

PHILIP: I shall find out and you shall be punished!!

FERDINAND: (*Entering, rubbing his hands.*) What a terrible fucking country! I'm freezing half to death.

ISABELLA: We were told that Philip was here in these chambers. Who are you, his valet?

FERDINAND: Must be a huge advantage to be so corpulent in this climate.

PHILIP: This is an outrage!

ISABELLA: (*Through clenched teeth.*) Where…is…the…boy?

PHILIP: If you do not leave this place immediately I will have you taken away and chopped into pieces!

ISABELLA: If *you* do not leave this place immediately I will burn you alive!

PHILIP: I'll have your head on a spike!

ISABELLA: I will turn you to coal!

PHILIP: Ravens will peck out your eyeballs!

ISABELLA: Your flesh will be dust. It will blow in the wind.

FERDINAND: (*Laughing.*) Let us perhaps try to resolve this without resorting to mindless violence.

ISABELLA: (*To FERDINAND.*) I feel a horrible fury brewing. Feel my palm.

FERDINAND: (*Doing so.*) It sweats like a fishmonger's.

ISABELLA takes out a small portrait and hands it to him. She waits expectantly as he examines it.

PHILIP: This is indeed Isabella of Spain. This, if you must know, is the woman who is soon to become my mother-in-law.

FERDINAND: I beg your pardon?

PHILIP: Yes. Isabella has here that wonderful, contradictory blend of haughtiness and humility, of serenity and severity. She is no looker, of course, but there is something about her here which commands… respect.

ISABELLA: (*Severely.*) So…respect her now.

PHILIP: (*Laughing heartily.*) You are asking me to believe that this middle-aged trout standing before me now is the self same woman as this dignified woman who instils fear, devotion and hatred throughout the known globe?

FERDINAND: You have just signed your own death warrant.

PHILIP: (*Laughing.*) And who might you be, Grandpapa?

FERDINAND: King Ferdinand.

PHILIP: (*Laughing.*) A veritable double-act then!

FERDINAND: Of Castile and Aragon.

PHILIP: (*Laughing, a mock bow.*) So…where are your crowns, my decrepit Majesties? Where, tell me, are your crowns of gold and fire?

Slowly and with solemnity, ISABELLA and FERDINAND produce their crowns. Regal music. They slowly lower them onto their heads. PHILIP's laughter peters out. In a sudden moment of understanding, he drops to his knees.

I bid you welcome, your Majesties, to our happy little

court.

ISABELLA: Stand up.

He rises.

(*Matter of fact.*) You must now die of course because it would be absurd of me to let this go, especially after the insults you have thrown at us but also because it is a capital offence to impersonate royalty who, as I am sure you are well aware, are God's representatives on earth.

PHILIP: I am impersonating no-one…

ISABELLA: You are no longer required to talk. I shall find out your identity from the Emperor.

PHILIP: I am his son.

ISABELLA: Do you want your death to be long and drawn out?

PHILIP: I am Philip. I am the man you are looking for.

ISABELLA takes out another small portrait from her cloak. Hands it to him.

ISABELLA: This…this is Philip the Fair.

PHILIP: And that is me.

FERDINAND and ISABELLA look at each other and both laugh.

Why are you laughing?

ISABELLA: This man looks like a god. He is slim and healthy and he is the epitome of male beauty.

PHILIP: It is me.

FERDINAND and ISABELLA both laugh.

Why are you laughing?

ISABELLA: You both dress like fairies, I grant you, but there the likeness ends.

PHILIP: I swear to you, before God and the Pope and all that is true, that I am Philip of Burgundy, son of the Emperor Maximilian, the man who is to marry Juana of Castile.

ISABELLA strikes him.

ISABELLA: (*To FERDINAND.*) Bring in the painter, Enriquez.

FERDINAND: (*Calling off.*) Enriquez the Painter!

ISABELLA: Enriquez is Spain's finest portrait artist and he has travelled here with us. He is the man who created these paintings.

PHILIP: Yes. We became brothers in ale.

LOUTS: (*Off.*) In ale!!!

ENRIQUEZ comes on. He prostrates himself.

ENRIQUEZ: Your Majesties…

ISABELLA: The function of the artist is the representation of fact. Yes? To act as witness to history?

ENRIQUEZ: Yes, Majesty.

ISABELLA: To reproduce scenes from real life and to paint as he finds?

ENRIQUEZ: Of course, Majesty.

ISABELLA: Invention is not required.

ENRIQUEZ: He must stick to the facts.

ISABELLA: For the facts are sacred. I am so glad we're agreed.

ENRIQUEZ: Always agreed, Majesty.

ISABELLA: Now…do you know this wretch?

ENRIQUEZ is silent.

I do believe I asked you a question.

ENRIQUEZ: Yes, Majesty.

A silence.

FERDINAND: Then identify the fucker!!!

ENRIQUEZ: (*Terrified.*) This…is…Prince Philip…son of the Emperor…Maximilian, Majesty.

A long silence.

FERDINAND: Darling?

ISABELLA: (*Closing her eyes.*) One moment, please.

FERDINAND: Oh dear, dear, dear.

ENRIQUEZ: Your Majesty…?

FERDINAND: Do you have a wife, Enriquez?

ENRIQUEZ: Yes, Majesty.

FERDINAND: And children?

ENRIQUEZ: Three, Majesty.

FERDINAND: Oh, that *is* sad.

They all watch ISABELLA as she inwardly wrestles with her fury.

ENRIQUEZ: (*Desperately.*) If you would allow me a word in my defence…it is common practice these days amongst portrait painters, who are after all merely satisfying the needs and the desires of their customers… rather than being granted the freedom to…to follow the dictates of their own imaginations…which would of course be nice…it is common practice sometimes to… sometimes to…how can I describe it… to be asked to…

to... disregard certain physical features of those who are sitting for them. In the case of Philip here he...urged me, with yes a small financial inducement I confess... to create flesh which hugged the bone, the skeleton... a touch more tightly than you see it does in actuality. And, if I might make so bold...since I see that I may here be defending my very life with this speech...when I painted your own portrait you also were keen for me not to...not to...well, you instructed me to...smooth out the forehead, to lift the bust, to straighten the nose, to whiten the complexion, to make dainty the wrist, render the frown less severe, the...

ISABELLA lets out a furious scream which lasts for quite some time.

Then silence.

ISABELLA: You have painted your last untruth. You have created your final lie.

ENRIQUEZ: Philip... Please?!!!

PHILIP: Your Majesty, might I say that Enriquez is a wonderful talent and he is surely only a victim of the desperate economic situation in which all artists unhappily find themselves and I do hope that some mercy might be...

ISABELLA: I want this man garrotted for his dishonest creations!

FERDINAND kicks ENRIQUEZ out, whimpering.

A long, embarrassed silence.

(Not looking at PHILIP.) So...what can I say? I suppose it's...I suppose it has to be...welcome to the family then.

She holds out her hand for him to kiss.

PHILIP goes down on one knee and kisses it.

PHILIP: (*With deference.*) The family.

Scene 4

LUDO enters, polishing a sword. ANGELINA comes on after him.

ANGELINA: Ludo, I do not know the reason for living... the family?

LUDO: Family is nothing.

ANGELINA: And love.

LUDO: Just go.

ANGELINA: I have done nothing but love.

LUDO: Your love is a pollution.

ANGELINA: My love is holy. It is God's love.

LUDO: Your aspirations are limited to the folding of clothing and the preparation of suppers.

ANGELINA: Ludo, please. You are plotting something.

LUDO: 'Ludo, please. You are plotting something.' What have you become?

ANGELINA: We must be...practical. We must survive.

LUDO: I will ram your pragmatism down your throat and watch you gag on it!

ANGELINA: Your hatred is too...

LUDO: You used to have some fire in your belly, used to have some rage in your soul.

ANGELINA: I have rage.

LUDO: Yours was a beautiful rage.

ANGELINA: It's no way to live.

LUDO: Our mother's spirit demands justice and my death will be a glorious one.

ANGELINA: Why all this talk of dying?

LUDO: You walk like a Christian, strutting, with your buttocks clenched, in a blind terror of farting, and now your nose is elevated, as if looking down might bring you closer to the gutter from where you sprang. You talk like a Christian, with your clipped prissy syllables. I have seen the way you eat. Like the princesses, with your little finger cocked. Yes, you are manufactured. A black heart in a white mask.

ANGELINA: What is happening to you?

LUDO: Just go. Let me polish this steel. Steel which they will use no doubt to sever black throats.

ANGELINA: If you will not be my brother, Ludo, then yes...I would rather die.

LUDO: Go dig your grave then.

ANGELINA: Your heart is so hard...

LUDO: They denied me my boyhood. They denied me my days in the sun, playing with balls, running after animals, chasing the girls. Do they believe that crimes in hot countries will be so easily forgotten? But when you stamp on a cockroach you give birth to a thousand more. You murder a man in his tent and when his sons become men they will come looking for you. They will drag you from your palaces, defile your bejewelled bitches and they will pluck out your hearts. And now I am a man. My mother...

ANGELINA: (*In tears.*) She was *our* mother, Ludo. *Our* mother.

LUDO: I saw it. She begged them, begged them to spare her. But they...they...

ANGELINA: They laughed, yes!

LUDO: Even as they stuffed their balls back into their breeches they laughed!

ANGELINA: But the killing must stop.

LUDO: And revenge… it must be upon the innocent.

ANGELINA: What are you saying?

LUDO: And yet the innocent do not exist.

ANGELINA: But I…I am innocent!

LUDO: You are wasting your tears, Angelina. Save them for the cat with the thorn in its paw or the little caged bird that has broken its wing.

ANGELINA: I cannot bear to be in the same room as you when you…

LUDO: Then go, go, go!

JUANA: (*Entering in bridal gown. She looks stunning.*) I have been looking for you both! You have been avoiding me! Angelina…?

ANGELINA: (*Exiting, upset.*) My lady…

LUDO: My lady.

JUANA: She is so tearful of late.

LUDO: Most tearful.

JUANA: So…how do I look?

LUDO: You look…nice, my lady.

JUANA: Do you mean it? Nice? Nice, you think?

LUDO: Nice.

JUANA: (*Spinning.*) Tell me what you think. Will I be a hit? Say.

LUDO: You look...

JUANA: Come on, Ludo, you know I value your opinion. Expand a little.

LUDO: I am no expert in the field of female fashion.

JUANA: (*Laughing.*) Then flatter me, boy!

LUDO: Help me.

JUANA: I think you have chosen extremely well, my lady.

LUDO: Yes.

JUANA: The dress accentuates your figure whilst at the same time it displays the correct amount of modesty.

LUDO: Yes.

JUANA: Modesty that is most fitting for a Christian princess.

LUDO: Just so.

JUANA: My bust is not too showy?

LUDO: Not at all.

JUANA: Because I believe the idea is to demonstrate to all those in attendance that I am a woman who, beyond this virginal white, has breasts that are just throbbing and bursting to produce milk for the next generation of empire.

LUDO: I see you have quickly come round to the idea of this marriage.

JUANA: It was Jesus.

LUDO: Jesus?

JUANA: He spoke to me.

LUDO: And the Devil?

JUANA: He spoke to me also.

LUDO: And they are of the same opinion?

JUANA: Oh, Alfonso is such a tease. He does laugh at me, as you know. But I see now that it's all for the best.

LUDO: And anyway you have no choice.

JUANA: That's true enough, my Ludo. Come and give me a hug then. Congratulate me.

LUDO: On what, my lady?

JUANA: On my betrothal, silly!

LUDO: I feel I cannot... I have no affection for you. I must have none.

JUANA: Why won't you look at me?

LUDO: (*Head down, upset.*) Because I am in such a torment when I do.

JUANA: There is no man on this earth I love more than you. I have a nagging love for my father, of course, but he doesn't deserve it. He has not earned it. He assumes it as all fathers do. But you...

LUDO: Juana...you must know how much knowing you has benefited me.

JUANA: I would hope so.

LUDO: Without your love and protection I would have been a corpse long ago.

JUANA: Why all these wild words?

LUDO: I long for release from this...hell.

JUANA: What do you mean, hell? This is Spain. This is the centre of the universe.

LUDO: Where the fire burns the hottest.

JUANA: Look at me, Ludo.

He slowly brings his head round to her.

You look so severe. That playful quality in your gaze, the one I have cherished since I was a girl, it has quite vanished.

LUDO: (*Advancing towards her.*) The playfulness has been a...pretence.

JUANA: Why is it that I suddenly feel extremely scared of you.

LUDO: Because I am about to commit a terrible act.

JUANA: A terrible act?

LUDO: One which I have been preparing to commit all my life.

JUANA: I don't understand a word you...

LUDO: And it is made all the more terrible because it must be perpetrated upon the only thing I can say that I care for.

JUANA: You have the look of a...

LUDO: This is for my people, for my mother...I am left with no alternative.

JUANA: Have you been drinking or...?

LUDO: (*Approaching her, menacingly.*) Whatever happiness I have experienced has been because of you. I can recall the occasional act of generosity, the merest touch of kindness. A soft word, an intimate gesture. And making music together. I would show off to you a little, my clumsy hands over the keyboard, making you laugh. Playing the fool for you. Sometimes as a boy I daydreamed that we could be married. Run off to a desert island and live a life of simplicity. I would hunt animals. We would eat by the fire with our fine little mulattos playing at our feet. The sea would kiss the shore and the huge African sun would sink into the ocean. Yes, every night the same and we at peace with this regularity. And the golden glow on our faces. From the fire. And from the sun. We would exchange sweet looks, all words redundant, a smile from me to you and from you to me. A recognition of our bliss. And that we deserved our bliss because, Juana, we were intelligent and peaceful and we lived our lives so well. Without our gods, perhaps. With just our animals and our herbs and my cooking and the sea.

Suddenly she jumps up onto him, wrapping her legs around him, kissing him wildly.

JUANA: Oh my God, Ludo! I want you, I want you, I want you!

LUDO: (*Stunned.*) What?

JUANA: If you must, just do it! Just do it! Just do it!

LUDO: You don't understand!

JUANA: Do it now! Do it now! I have wanted you for so long, boy! So just…

LUDO: But this is to be my revenge! My life's meaning!

JUANA: Quickly!

LUDO: You must not be all…acquiescence.

JUANA: Quickly!

LUDO: No, you must not collude in your own destruction.

Lights go down on them and come up on ARDILLES at a desk.

ANGELINA comes on.

ARDILLES: And so what can I do for you?

45

ANGELINA: I am unhappy.

ARDILLES: Yes?

ANGELINA: And I am tired of it.

ARDILLES: You are unhappy and you are tired of it? But you are a servant, yes?

ANGELINA: Yes.

ARDILLES: And so therefore your happiness is…?

ANGELINA: Irrelevant, yes.

ARDILLES: But anyway describe your symptoms for me. It will be useful to glean a little knowledge of such matters and it will satisfy my professional curiosity.

ANGELINA: There is a constant, hollow aching here. A tightness.

ARDILLES: (*Writing.*) In your chest?

ANGELINA: My work is tedious. I am not valued at all, either financially or emotionally, and it is clear that I contribute nothing to society, to the happiness of my fellows.

ARDILLES: Yes, yes… Just as I suspected.

ANGELINA: I would be happy to work hard in life but my labour has been sold to the system which exploits me. I would like to form an association with others in a similar position. Find a voice together to defend ourselves from those who profit from our daily grind.

ARDILLES: Just as I suspected, yes.

ANGELINA: Also I am full of a hatred which I try to suppress since I find it ugly and debasing. I know violence is wrong but sometimes I want to smash items in the kitchen.

ARDILLES: Go on.

ANGELINA: And once…

ARDILLES: Yes?

ANGELINA: Once I even spat in the tureen.

ARDILLES: (*Writing.*) Spat…in…the…tureen.

ANGELINA: I know women who sell their bodies and
who earn more in a day than I do in half a year.

ARDILLES: But this is immoral, no?

ANGELINA: Yes.

ARDILLES: Though you could of course do rather well.

ANGELINA: I am unhappy, doctor, and I am tired of it.
I long to spend my days outside a hut, pounding millet
for my children. If the hut was my own and the millet I
had picked myself.

ARDILLES: I shall be candid with you, my dear. I desire
coloureds. And, of course, you are a most desirable
coloured. And why do I desire women of the darker
hue? It is because coloured women are simply more…
frolicsome. More liberated twixt the sheets, as it were.
They do not confuse sex with morality. The insertion
of the male member into the female *wagina* and the
movements subsequent to this penetration need not
only exist as a means of producing offspring. God
intended coitus to be both exciting and pleasurable.
And this the white man and the coloured woman
understand well. I am also a man who suffers from low
self-esteem and a most unsightly limp. This makes me
unattractive to the quality females of my own race. I do
appeal however to females from the lower economic
strata as to them I wield a great power…all things being
relative of course. My wife, for instance, is rotund, from
the lower orders and is happy only when her already

47

ample guts are bulging with the unborn. I am a good lover, I am told, if a little over-anxious at times. (*Hands her a piece of paper.*) Come to my chambers at any hour and for just a small section of your day I will see you remunerated well. Also I have a tongue which is as long and as agile as a lizard's and who knows…this may even put a smile upon your sweet sullen face. Thank you and with that I shall bid you good day.

A loud, anguished scream from JUANA.

Lights down and then back up on JUANA and LUDO. They lie in silence.

JUANA: What have we done?

LUDO: (*Standing.*) And so…my life is over.

JUANA: (*In a daze.*) Ludo…what have you done to me? (*A silence.*) You have… ruined…my dress.

LUDO: Yes. This is now the end of me.

He slowly leaves, passing ANGELINA on his way out.

ANGELINA gradually takes in what she sees.

ANGELINA: My lady!!

JUANA: (*Holding up her dress.*) He has, you know. He has completely ruined my dress.

Scene 5

JUANA stands on a chair in her bridal gown, while ANGELINA busies herself with the dress. ISABELLA is doing some embroidery, while FERDINAND paces about with a ledger open. LUDO is standing to attention close by.

ISABELLA: And so, Juana, to recap: since I *am* a woman,

albeit a hugely powerful woman, I still adhere to the principle that my first duty, after God of course, is to my husband. Even if the said husband is a compulsive fatherer of bastards.

FERDINAND: (*Laughing.*) Not in front of the children, please.

ISABELLA: However, so long as one partner remains faithful then I believe that God will indulge you.

FERDINAND: In that He is most gracious.

ISABELLA: A new bride must display at all times patience, modesty and tolerance. Men, as you must have by now discovered, are frightful bores so learn the art of nodding and smiling. However, whenever he is discussing affairs of state, you must be more alert for this, darling, is your opportunity to influence his political choices.

FERDINAND: Manipulate the fucker, darling!

ISABELLA: So that his actions always benefit…

ISABELLA/FERDINAND: Spain!

ISABELLA: I do not think your future husband's intellect anywhere near on a par with your own so one would assume that this will not be too difficult. Are you listening?

JUANA opens her mouth to speak but no words come.

As you are no doubt aware my own intelligence far surpasses that of your father but still we have been able to construct a stable marriage, this disparity notwithstanding.

FERDINAND: (*Moving away.*) Now…Ludo. I want your opinion on something.

LUDO steps forward to FERDINAND, while ISABELLA continues to address her daughter.

You will remember our little chat about the Jews?

LUDO: Yes, sire.

FERDINAND: And you will remember that some years ago we made them wear that sign on their clothes so we could pick the buggers out from the crowd? And that we shoved them into their ghettos so we knew where they were?

LUDO: Yes, sire.

FERDINAND: Well, now…now we have, it seems, run out of 'em.

ISABELLA: Now… a wife can serve her man and her nation best if she makes friends with her stove as soon in the marriage as she can. Your husband will spend a lot of time away fighting so he will need good food inside him whenever he is home. Are you listening, darling?

JUANA opens her mouth to speak but no words come.

LUDO: Mission accomplished then, sire.

FERDINAND: Yes, but hold on a moment. We also stopped them practising as doctors, architects, and teachers.

LUDO: Yes, sire.

FERDINAND: The upshot being that Spain now has no doctors, architects or teachers.

LUDO: I see.

ISABELLA: Always ensure that your husband, especially during his military campaigns, has at his finger tips complete changes of linen. Are you listening, darling?

JUANA opens her mouth to speak but no words come.

FERDINAND: Our people fall sick, they die where they drop, our new buildings fall down from a gust from the sea, our schools are full of dunces fit only for the armed services.

ISABELLA: Your husband will on occasions expect congress and to this you must submit graciously. You will find it a minor inconvenience but without regular bouts he will become moody, depressive and oftentimes violent. Find your pleasure through more spiritual pursuits and do not submit to jealousy if he strays. Be thankful you are at least temporarily being spared such an onerous prodding. Are you listening, darling?

JUANA opens her mouth to speak but no words come.

LUDO: Perhaps then you have gone too far?

FERDINAND: Spanish science and Spanish culture are dying on their feet! Our schools and our hospitals, our universities and our markets, our banks and our businesses – all grinding to a halt. What is more: we need Jewish loot to fight the French and to keep the Islamic hordes at bay. The question then: what do we do?

LUDO: You are asking me, sire?

ISABELLA: Finally, darling, it must be said that anything you might do in the interests of the state can only be deemed right and proper. In every thought and in every deed you must serve your homeland.

JUANA opens her mouth to speak but no words come.

ANGELINA bursts into tears.

FERDINAND: (*To LUDO.*) For goodness sake, why is this sister of yours always crying?

ANGELINA: Forgive me.

FERDINAND: (*To ANGELINA.*) Perhaps you spend too much time with your mistress. Both of you are such sensitive flowers!

ISABELLA: Now the French will no longer let us pass through the Orleans' lands so you shall have to travel by sea. We have armed a fleet at Tortosa to take you to Flanders. The country's gone into the red, Juana, for your little party so do remember to smile throughout.

FERDINAND: (*To ANGELINA.*) Try not to give in to every minor upset, my dear.

ISABELLA: The holds of these thirty ships will contain biscuits of Seville and of Jerez, olive oil, salt, and delicious preserves from Betanzos and Galicia.

FERDINAND: Is it that you feel that life is unfair?

ISABELLA: There will be twenty thousand barrels of ordinary wine, four hundred of high-quality wine, three hundred wineskins full of drinking water...

FERDINAND: (*To ANGELINA.*) You think God's bounty dished out disproportionately?

ISABELLA: ...a huge amount of dried beef and salted pork, two hundred rams, twenty cows...

FERDINAND: (*To ANGELINA.*) That the few live beautifully, while the many must rot?

ISABELLA: ...a thousand chickens, ten thousand eggs, a hundred thousand salted herrings...

FERDINAND: (*To ANGELINA.*) Is this why the tears course down your cheeks?

ISABELLA: ...twelve thousand cod, five hundred barrels of vinegar...

FERDINAND: (*To ANGELINA.*) This is, one fears, the way of the world.

ISABELLA: And three hundred barrels of butter and lard.

FERDINAND: (*To ANGELINA.*) And things, I'm afraid, are unlikely to change.

ISABELLA: Now, you will be stopping at Portland, England, where I have prepared crates of gifts for you to pass onto King Henry and his unfortunately rather hook-nosed little consort. One trusts they will be mightily impressed when they see our beautiful boats, these bog-dwelling Tudors!

FERDINAND: (*To ANGELINA.*) If we all wept like you at the drop of a hat, the world would be constantly awash with tears. It would be like Noah's Flood all over again! Isn't that right, Ludo?

LUDO smiles.

ANGELINA stops crying.

ANGELINA: (*Suddenly very serious.*) I shall never…ever… weep again.

ISABELLA: Now…are there any questions?

JUANA opens her mouth to speak but no words come.

I do hope you've been listening, darling. A mother can only dispense advice like this once in a daughter's lifetime.

JUANA: (*With great difficulty.*) I know that the whole of the civilised world is now focusing its attention upon this wedding and even upon this very room. I know how important it is for the lands of both Spain and Flanders to unite and face down the unruly French. I know that the future of Catholicism is riding upon these slender shoulders of mine. You have been good parents. I could not expect more than you have given me: an education, a love of literature and an unswerving faith in the Lord our God. Perhaps you might have listened to my views more often but I know you are both busy people. And this moment, I know, has been coming since I was a baby. But I have to tell you…something terrible has happened, something catastrophic, an act of terrorism which has destroyed me forever. You have to know, my parents, that this marriage can now no longer take place.

A long silence.

LUDO shifts his position.

After a while FERDINAND bursts out laughing. The company watch him. His laughter soon becomes uncontrollable.

LUDO has to help him stand.

Then ISABELLA too begins to laugh. Soon both monarchs are clutching their sides, weeping with laughter.

Why are you laughing at me? Please! Mother, Father! Stop laughing at me! You are always, everyone is always laughing at me! Please!

The laughter continues.

Something dreadful has happened! I am your daughter! It is now impossible for me to marry! You have to listen to me! I am serious! This is not a joke! I am not joking!

The laughter continues for some time.

(*A mighty scream.*) Please will you all stop this constant fucking laughter!!!!!

FERDINAND and ISABELLA are shocked out of their hysterics. As they calm down, they watch their daughter.

A terrible crime has been committed. Not just against me but against the whole of Spain. At present I *am* the whole of Spain and I demand justice. I demand justice immediately. Whoever dares to violate the authority of Spain must be destroyed. I am now unable to marry. Now...pay attention and I will try to speak the thing I must speak without falling apart.

Suddenly ALFONSO appears on his cross.

Oh, go away.

FERDINAND and ISABELLA look at each other.

Go away. I am going to say it!

ALFONSO: But you gave yourself to him!

JUANA: But I cannot...the act...the act itself...

ALFONSO: Your animal passion, your...

ISABELLA: Juana?

JUANA: I cannot... The act...the act!

FERDINAND: What act?

ISABELLA: Juana?

ALFONSO: He will suffer for your crime.

JUANA: But I must say!

ALFONSO: This marriage is necessary.

JUANA: But how can I...

ALFONSO: We must unite.

JUANA: But my life is now over!

ALFONSO: Say it was a stranger raped you.

JUANA: A stranger raped me?!

FERDINAND/ISABELLA: What???

ALFONSO: The highest bliss lies in negation of the self.

JUANA: But my wedding night! How can I...?

FERDINAND: What the hell is she talking about?

ISABELLA: Juana, you must be ill! Call in that physician from La Coruna!

FERDINAND: (*Exiting, calling.*) That physician from La Coruna!!

ISABELLA: Ludo, help her down from there.

LUDO approaches JUANA.

JUANA: Don't let him anywhere near me!!!!

ISABELLA: I command you, as your mother and as your queen, that you calm yourself down this very instant!

JUANA steps down from the chair. She walks forward uncertainly.

JUANA: Last night...last night...last night...

ISABELLA: Last night, yes?

JUANA: (*Pointing to LUDO.*) This man...this man...

ISABELLA: This is Ludo whom we all know and love, yes?

JUANA: This man...

ISABELLA: As one of the family.

JUANA: This man came to me...

ISABELLA: (*To LUDO.*) What *is* she talking about? This really is becoming a frightful bore.

JUANA: He came to me...

ISABELLA: (*Impatiently.*) Yes-yes, yes-yes...

JUANA: And he stole away...my innocence.

A silence.

ISABELLA: And how did he do that exactly?

JUANA: He...he...he... (*She begins to cry.*)

ISABELLA: (*To LUDO.*) And how did you do that?

LUDO: I think, your Majesty, what she is trying to say is
that we...

ALFONSO: (*Re-appearing.*) He told you about all the
poverty.

JUANA: He told me about all the poverty!

ISABELLA: What poverty?

ALFONSO: The children dying.

JUANA: He told me about all the children dying!

ALFONSO: The starvation, the droughts.

ISABELLA: I really don't begin to understand what all
this...

JUANA: Children dying and starvation and droughts
and...

ISABELLA: This mawkish nonsense again, is it?

ALFONSO: We all quietly accept...

JUANA: Conquest and murder...

ALFONSO: ...conquest and murder.

JUANA: Columbus and the Arawaks.

ALFONSO: Massacre in the Bahamas.

JUANA: In the Bahamas, massacre!

ALFONSO: (*Disappearing.*) The liquidation of the innocent
in the name of trade!!

JUANA: Liquidation of the innocent...of the innocent, he told me!

ISABELLA: Thank you, thank you. That's enough. You *are* peculiar. You are sick. Quite clearly. And now I'm rather looking forward to being shot of you.

JUANA: Mother...

ISABELLA: Yes?

JUANA: I am so... So very... (*She breaks down.*)

ISABELLA: Do you know how important all this is? To me, to your father, to Spain? God has cursed me by giving me daughters and so I must turn this horror to my advantage by using you all as exchange goods. I have skilfully negotiated blood pacts with all the major powers on the continent. In twenty years I shall have the pleasure of seeing my children and grandchildren on every throne in Europe. Isabella I betrothed to the heir of the Portuguese throne, Catherine to Arthur the Prince of England and you I have tied to the Flemish throne. We now have France completely surrounded, totally isolated. I don't want you, Juana, to jeopardise it all with your socialistic sensitivities!

FERDINAND comes back on with ARDILLES, the physician. We see he has a limp.

Ah, there you are. Good. This girl is showing signs of mental distress. Cure her or die.

ARDILLES: Of course, Majesty.

He goes to JUANA and puts his hand on her forehead.

Yes, yes, just as I suspected.

He puts his hand on her wrist.

Yes, yes, just as I suspected.

58

He puts his hand on her neck.

And might I ask her exact date of birth?

ISABELLA: The sixth of November in the year of our Lord 1479.

ARDILLES: And the place?

ISABELLA: Toledo.

He takes an astrological instrument from his pocket and begins to examine the heavens.

ARDILLES: Yes, yes, just as I suspected.

ISABELLA: What is it?

ARDILLES: She is sick. Sick with love. And though she has not yet met her beau I am of the opinion that, the moment she does, her ailments will disappear and her behaviour will immediately return to normal.

There is a long silence.

ARDILLES looks nervously from the king to the queen.

ISABELLA cogitates.

ARDILLES sinks to his knees in desperation.

Your Majesty, I...

ISABELLA: Thank you.

FERDINAND: Thank you.

JUANA: (*After a pause.*) Thank...you.

ARDILLES chokes back a sob of relief.

Scene 6

A balcony. A celebratory crowd scream their enthusiasm. JUANA stands with a fixed smile, waving regally. She faces forward throughout. ANGELINA by her side.

JUANA: So…to begin with they will pluck out his fingernails one by one. I have never seen so many people, Angelina! My thoughts are in such a fuddle. What is your estimate?

ANGELINA: Ten thousand?

JUANA: How is my waving?

ANGELINA: Perfect, my lady.

JUANA: I think they approve. (*Breaking.*) They will think me a…common slut, Angelina.

ANGELINA: On his behalf I beg forgiveness.

JUANA: (*Recovering.*) Then they will slowly saw off the stumps of his hands.

ANGELINA: Imprison him but please…spare his life.

JUANA: (*Breaking.*) Even the word, it's so… Slut. Slut. Slut. (*Recovering.*) They will then carve the sign of the cross into his chest. Note how I maintain this counter-clockwise motion of the wrist, endeavouring to put as little strain as possible on the fragile muscles in my hand.

ANGELINA: Could you not say that some villain gained access to you and violated you in this way?

JUANA: You think my smile insincere?

ANGELINA: You have perfect teeth, my lady.

JUANA: His body, while he is still alive, will then be lowered into a cauldron of boiling fat.

PHILIP: (*Stepping onto the balcony, the screaming increasing as he does.*) At last we meet!!

JUANA: May I help you?

PHILIP: How I have been dreaming of this moment! And may I say that I am not in the least displeased by what I see. You look ravishing! (*Pause.*) Who is the African?

JUANA: My lady-in-waiting. Do you object?

PHILIP: No but I have simply never been quite this close to a coloured before.

JUANA: You may go.

ANGELINA curtsies and leaves. PHILIP lustfully watches her go. After a while.

PHILIP: (*Snapping out of it.*) You must understand…I have nothing at all against these people.

JUANA: Of course.

PHILIP: I see you prefer the anti-clockwise action, do you? Is that a Spanish custom?

JUANA: I don't know.

PHILIP: And they tell me, Juana, that you are very learned. This I admire greatly. My tutors were always exasperated by my indolence. You will discover over time that I delight more in the gratification of the senses, the appetites of the body, than in the ephemeral pleasures of the intellect.

JUANA: I could not live without my books.

PHILIP: And yet the true subject has no need for the written word.

JUANA: It seems he must till the soil rather than study the scriptures.

PHILIP: Tend the animals and maintain the vineyards.

JUANA: Sweat in the foundries and people the armies.

PHILIP: Let the priests assure the common man of God's

will. You have stopped waving.

JUANA: Ah yes. (*She resumes.*)

PHILIP: I do believe that we are going to get along swimmingly.

JUANA: I hope so. Life is long.

PHILIP: But for our adoring flag-wavers down here it is not quite so. One is lucky to get two decades of work out of any one of them!

JUANA: They die young in these parts?

PHILIP: Most of them are in their graves by thirty-five.

JUANA: Do they eat enough oily fish?

PHILIP: They live largely on barley and root vegetables.

JUANA: Sometimes I wonder how they can love us so much when they suffer as they do.

PHILIP: We are continuity, my lady.

JUANA: I lack the common touch.

PHILIP: (*Laughing.*) It will not be necessary to touch them, my lady!

JUANA: When one laughs one is divorced from God. One is separate from existence. It is an act laced with misanthropy.

PHILIP: And when one cries?

JUANA: Perhaps one moves closer to Him through pain.

PHILIP: (*Laughing.*) Well, I'm afraid I'm a laugher, Juana.

JUANA: (*Breaking.*) And I a crier.

PHILIP: And so we complement each other perfectly! I…

love you.

JUANA: Our acquaintance has been brief.

PHILIP: I realise I must be a disappointment to you. I have indulged myself. Of course I have. And this I know is a terrible abuse of privilege. The prince stuffs himself in revelry and gluttony, his distended gut straining at his breeches, while the scrawny paupers drop in the fields where they dig. This is no doubt wrong.

JUANA: When so many in the world are starving it is surely a sin to be so...obese.

PHILIP: I have been starved of affection, Juana. Starved of love and so I have sought comfort through excessive consumption. Your love will thin me down.

JUANA: I will...love you.

PHILIP: My parents...always so distant.

JUANA: They never listened?

PHILIP: Never listened.

JUANA: Your personality has not been nurtured?

PHILIP: They have expected me to toe the line.

JUANA: Unquestioningly.

PHILIP: Oh so unquestioningly.

JUANA: Yours has been a childhood of isolation.

PHILIP: I cannot relate to others.

JUANA: The radical hate us for the softness of our upbringings.

PHILIP: I feel my loneliness is evaporating.

JUANA: Mine also.

PHILIP: I feel a communion with your soul.

JUANA: We are as one.

PHILIP: I feel tearful.

JUANA: So tearful.

> *He slowly holds his hand out towards her.*
>
> *She slowly brings hers up to his.*
>
> *The crowd approve.*

PHILIP: Tonight I promise I will be…gentle.

> *JUANA sobs.*

My love?

> *She recovers.*

PHILIP: You have stopped waving.

JUANA: Ah. (*She resumes.*)

PHILIP: The moment of our union tonight promises me such rapture that it seems I have scarcely deserved such an honour.

JUANA: I have to tell you that I… I hope you will not be…

PHILIP: Since I first saw your portrait, Juana…I hope I can be candid…I have been so appallingly in love with you that…

JUANA: I think Enriquez complimented me.

PHILIP: No coloured oils could ever do you justice.

JUANA: You are making me blush.

PHILIP: May I kiss you?

JUANA: But…your people.

PHILIP: They are *our* people now.

JUANA: Our people. Will they approve?

PHILIP: Oh yes, Juana, they will. And besides…for them we are merely…entertainment.

JUANA looks to him. She smiles. He goes down on one knee. She touches his hair gently. The crowd scream their approval.

Slowly PHILIP stands. He moves towards her. Nervously they begin to kiss. It is gentle and tender. As their lips meet, the crowd falls silent. The kiss continues in silence.

Then a spontaneous burst of delight from the crowd. It is a deafening roar and it builds as the kiss continues.

Scene 7

LUDO alone. He holds a sword to his heart. He is attempting to run himself through. Shouts from the street. He fails in his attempt.

LUDO: They are coming for you, Ludo. So be quick! Surely this is them coming. I have no time for all this deliberation. The will of the State must be done. Juana, Juana…you stole my crime from me and still I am certain you would have me suffer for it. But you are undone. And therefore the Queen is undone. And yet why do I not feel wholly avenged? It is because Isabella must die. To violate her daughter is not enough. But now I long to fly to my virgins, soar to my heaven. The passage there, what will it be? Nothing. One savage, searing pain perhaps, as steel rips through flesh, a little nausea, a struggling for breath, a weakness of the limbs, a spreading chill in the bones, this pathetic life dripping away in a scarlet stream on these sandy stones. A darkness descending? And then away from here into bliss. That is all, Ludo. And yet because I am unavenged will this be my fate? Will I not rather spend an eternity in freezing vapours, my spirit abandoned in the cold unloving universe, eternally excluded from the light?

I am in such an agony.

Shouts off, closer. Footsteps up stairs.

Ludo, do as the Romans did. It is time to leave forever this unhappy stage. (*He attempts to kill himself.*) Ah, what is this sickly force which is binding me to life? I lack the will to live and yet, it seems, I do not yet have the necessary desire for death.

FERDINAND and GRUNT enter.

FERDINAND: I charge thee, Grunt, to manacle this nigger!

GRUNT: He has a sword, Majesty.

FERDINAND: As do you.

GRUNT: But his is the larger.

FERDINAND: Then disarm the cunt.

GRUNT approaches LUDO and they circle each other.

This is to be your replacement, Ludo. He comes highly recommended but I do like to see these people fight before I commit. I should like it to the death, if you please.

GRUNT: But his sword is larger.

FERDINAND: Grunt, my man, you are far from impressing me.

GRUNT: You said he was a base and cowering slave.

FERDINAND: I want to hear less of the lip, man, and more of the clanking of blades. You are a murderer, Grunt.

A man used to scrapping.

GRUNT: They were women mostly. And I slit their gullets from behind.

FERDINAND: So shackle this man or it's the gallows for you.

GRUNT: Ah, fuck it!

GRUNT and LUDO fight viciously.

FERDINAND: (*Checking his appearance in a pocket mirror.*) It seems you have offended Juana. She will not marry unless we incarcerate you. She also says she wants you dead. We have tried to talk her round but to no avail. The girl is clearly insane. Unfortunately this wedding is too important for us to refuse her. What did you do, man? What did you say to her? You know how delicate she is.

GRUNT's sword goes flying from his hand.

GRUNT: Ah, fuck it!

LUDO has won the fight.

GRUNT lies, disarmed on the floor, LUDO with his sword to the man's throat.

LUDO looks to the King, who deliberates for a time.

FERDINAND: Kill him.

GRUNT whimpers.

LUDO makes ready to kill.

Wait a moment!

GRUNT whimpers.

The King cogitates.

No, go on then...kill him.

GRUNT whimpers.

LUDO makes ready to kill.

FERDINAND turns his back to them and begins combing his hair.

Try as I might I cannot watch these things. It's all the effluent, you see.

LUDO approaches FERDINAND from behind.

LUDO: (*Aside.*) Fate has sent me this last opportunity. My final chance to strike against the Empire and rest my troubled soul. I hate this man less than I should, he has spent decades kicking me, whipping me, defaming me and yet…he has been the only father I… No. He must die. (*Raises his sword above FERDINAND's head.*) This then, this one blow is for centuries of the unjustly killed. (*The sword stays where it is.*) Oh, what is wrong with me? Have I been corrupted by the poison of pity? Or does white man's blood flow in my veins? (*He drops the sword.*) I deserve now whatever brutality Spain may devise for me.

FERDINAND: The shit-for-brains despatched yet?

GRUNT now rises and puts chains around LUDO's wrists, who accepts them passively.

To tell you the truth I did have him down as rather a large-buttocked loser and, what is more, his breath was that of a toilet attendant.

He turns round to see LUDO manacled and GRUNT holding a sword to his neck in a conquering posture.

Ah. So something of a turnaround then?

Scene 8

A candlelit bedroom. Wedding bells sound. JUANA, veiled, enters in a state of manic excitement. ANGELINA behind.

JUANA: He is both gentle and strong, tender and vigorous. He has a simple intelligence but is eager to learn. (*Aside.*) I have minutes now to save myself! I think I might even be falling in love, Angelina. I do believe that Philip of Burgundy and Juana of Castile will indeed forge a partnership great enough to shoulder the burden of governance which destiny will one day place upon us. Oh goodness... I have started referring to myself in the third person already! But let it go, let it go. Tell me, how did I come across during the ceremony?

ANGELINA: You were...

JUANA: Did I demonstrate the necessary solemnity?

ANGELINA: ...magnificent.

JUANA: (*Aside. Breaking.*) But last week I swore it was Ludo that I loved. (*Recovering.*) And Philip? Do not the crowd simply adore him?

ANGELINA: They adored you.

JUANA: What do you make of my husband? He idolises me, I think? (*Aside.*) I am in such a confusion of despair and delight! Though I do feel happy but...But at the same time I am not! I am riddled with guilt since now poor Ludo lies in gaol. But what if he confesses our sin? It was me! Me! I sucked him into my soul. I drank down my own damnation. Something possessed me. The Devil inhabited me, yes. I was not responsible for that...bestial lust that... Yes, he must die. For the sake of the unity of the State. It is of course...what is the right word... regrettable but... Do I mean that? Oh, I know not what I say. (*To ANGELINA.*) Your demi-devil brother has ruined me, has robbed me of my joy tonight!!

ANGELINA: I beg you, for our years of friendship, to have mercy on a wayward boy. His rage has blinded him.

JUANA: He must pay for what he has done to me.

ANGELINA: Then my life is over too.

JUANA: Angelina, you do understand?

ANGELINA: Of course.

JUANA: Tell me. I have often wondered...it must be tiresome having to agree with me all of the time? Have I been always right in everything?

ANGELINA: It is not my place to...

JUANA: You have never wanted to scream out in a fury of injured sensibilities?

ANGELINA: You are an educated...

JUANA: The righteous indignation of the working classes?

ANGELINA: Whereas I...

JUANA: The animal rage of the eternally wronged?

ANGELINA: I want the world to live in peace.

A silence.

JUANA then bursts out laughing.

I want us all to be as one. To share the treasures of the world equally.

The laughter continues.

JUANA: (*Suppressing laughter.*) You really must live more in the world.

ANGELINA: My world is these walls.

JUANA: Oh, my thoughts are hurting me, they crash like rocks inside my skull, like shards of rubble. The voices, the voices.

ANGELINA: The voices?

JUANA: (*Suddenly very serious.*) Angelina, I want now to offer you your freedom.

ANGELINA: My freedom?

JUANA: I will buy you a house. Yes! At the end of the street by the harbour. (*Aside.*) This is a beautiful idea, Alfonso. I thank you for it! (*To her.*) The house will be modest but comfortable. But we must be quick! You can come and go as you please. You will remain in my employment and, yes, from now on you will receive a wage. You will live as a citizen and not as a slave. Your hours will be regular, though evidently I would need you first thing in the morning and last thing at night. But we must be quick! Come here. Let me embrace you.

ANGELINA walks towards JUANA. They embrace.

ANGELINA: I do not know how to be free.

JUANA: You can dine in restaurants, you can talk to whom you like. You will daily taste the delights of liberty. You will have a decent pension and a comfortable old age…

ANGELINA: That you could show me such kindness after my brother has done what he has done… I am quite overcome.

They continue the embrace.

JUANA: There is of course one small thing I must ask of you. One little service I require…

ANGELINA: I will do anything that…

JUANA: I need to…appropriate your maidenhood.

A silence.

Since I of course am damaged goods.

ANGELINA: I do not…understand.

JUANA: You will hide under the bed in a state of undress. He will come to me and we will prepare for the consummation. Already there is a mob of Belgians outside waiting for the presentation of the sheets. On my signal we will change places. I trust the failing light will easily disguise this deception. A few minutes later and your freedom will be secured. But we must be quick. He will be here in a moment and the doctor is already pacing outside this room.

ANGELINA: But I have sworn before my conscience, before God that I will enter paradise as a virgin. That no man will ever do to me what men did to my mother.

JUANA: But for me!

ANGELINA: I would take your place at the stake if I had to but this is monstrous!

JUANA: I beg you, Angelina! Think of what I offer you in return.

ANGELINA: What you offer me!?

JUANA: But this was your brother's doing! You are tainted by his trespass! You can now atone for his crime. What greater redress could there be? This act of devotion will save my life, my reputation!

ANGELINA: My lady, I beg you not to ask such a thing of me!

JUANA: (*Suddenly on her knees.*) Angelina, let me implore you! This is the most important occasion in a woman's life. And I am a princess. I have been born and raised simply as an item of trade. We are not so different. You perceive that I am free, that I live a life of luxury but it is not so! I can never act on my dreams nor follow the whims of my imagination! I am a walking hunk of flesh born to bind the empire and through which unborn emperors will pass. My womb will disgorge murderers and psychopaths and the spouses of murderers and psychopaths. This is my destiny! Had I more courage I would throw myself from this tower but God will not allow it! We have travelled thus far together. Our fates are linked. In saving me you save yourself! Otherwise I am lost! I am lost!

PHILIP: (*Off.*) Oh, Juana! Juana!

JUANA: He is coming! Please! This is the moment! This! This!

ANGELINA: I cannot!

JUANA: (*Sinking to the floor, sobbing.*) Then I am ruined.

PHILIP: (*Off.*) Oh, Juana! My sweet and tender bride, I come for you, I come!

JUANA: That my life should end with such horror!

PHILIP: (*Off.*) Juana! Are you ready for your handsome prince?

ANGELINA: (*Very serious, measured.*) Say you will free him. Promise me you will spare my brother!

JUANA: But he cannot live!

PHILIP: (*Off.*) Juana! Juana!

ANGELINA: Then I cannot help you.

PHILIP: (*Off.*) Oh, Juana! Juana! The moment has arrived, my darling! Ten thousand people are outside the castle, candles lit and with expectation hanging in the night air!

ANGELINA: Promise me. By all that is good in this world.

The crowd starts up a slow hand clap outside.

JUANA: You have my word.

ANGELINA disappears under the bed just as PHILIP enters.

The clapping now increases in volume and speed until the end of the scene.

PHILIP: My beautiful bride, let me look at you!

He walks towards her.

May I kiss you?

JUANA: You may.

PHILIP: Ah, the intoxicating promise of ecstasy but not the ecstasy itself, the idea of sheer pleasure but not the pleasure itself. Let us look deep into each other's eyes and lock this moment in our hearts and minds.

He lifts her veil.

They stare at each other for some time.

I can hold out no longer!

He kisses her wildly, passionately.

She responds.

They gravitate towards the bed. They collapse onto it.

The clapping builds outside.

JUANA: Philip, wait! I must blow out the candle.

PHILIP: But I want to see your flesh. To see it yield to my touch!

JUANA: I beg you!

PHILIP: (*Laughing.*) Oh, your sweet Spanish innocence!

JUANA rises from the bed and goes to the candle. She blows out the light.

Darkness falls.

ANGELINA comes out from under the bed and JUANA takes her place. ANGELINA approaches the bed.

My darling, come here!

ANGELINA gets into the bed.

As PHILIP and ANGELINA begin a light comes up on JUANA under the bed.

JUANA: Do not laugh. I know you are going to laugh.

ALFONSO appears above.

Do not torment me. Don't you think I am tormented enough?

ALFONSO: He is very…

JUANA: Please.

ALFONSO: …passionate.

JUANA: No more.

ALFONSO: And she of course is weeping.

JUANA: Yes.

ALFONSO: Rather touching.

JUANA: How he grunts like a creature!

ALFONSO: Not long to go now.

PHILIP bellows with relief.

The light fades on JUANA. She comes out from under the bed.

PHILIP: Thank you, my darling.

ANGELINA rises from the bed.

Juana, where are you going?

ANGELINA slips under the bed.

JUANA relights the candle.

JUANA: I want to see your face.

PHILIP: I am a man who is awash with peace and with joy and…

JUANA: It was the highlight of my life also.

A knock on the door.

PHILIP: Yes, we are done!

ARDILLES: (*Entering with a candle.*) The inspection of the sheets, your Majesties.

PHILIP: This custom is, it might be said, something of an intrusion upon one's intimacy.

ARDILLES comes to the bed and inspects the sheets.

ANGELINA lets out a sob under the bed.

What was that?

JUANA: I heard nothing.

ARDILLES: Yes, yes, just as I suspected.

The lights change.

The day breaks.

ARDILLES steps forward, flanked by PHILIP and JUANA.

A crowd cheers and roars in excitement.

PHILIP and JUANA smile and wave.

Ladies and gentlemen of the Empire, it is my honour and great privilege to present to you this couple, united in love to safeguard your interests and the stability of Europe. And so I call upon you now to enjoy this national holiday and to…REJOICE!!

A great fanfare of music and a huge blood-stained sheet is suddenly unfurled across the stage in celebration.

The crowd howls in happiness.

End of Act One.

ACT TWO

Scene 1

A large bed in which ISABELLA sleeps. FERDINAND and ARDILLES on either side of it. FERDINAND has received a blow. He does not speak for some time.

FERDINAND: Dying?

ARDILLES: Dying.

FERDINAND: Dying?

ARDILLES: Dying.

A silence.

FERDINAND: Dying?

ARDILLES: Dying.

FERDINAND: Dying?

ARDILLES: Dying.

A silence.

FERDINAND: Dying?

ARDILLES: Dying.

FERDINAND: Dying?

ARDILLES: I wish it were otherwise.

FERDINAND: But...she is the monarch.

ARDILLES: Yes.

FERDINAND: And is intimate with God. Are you are sure she is...

ARDILLES: Dying. Yes.

FERDINAND: But. This is… It can't… You see… (*He breaks off.*) Dying?

ARDILLES: Her breathing is laboured, she is slipping in and out of consciousness continually, her heartbeat is weak and erratic. She is in an agony of convulsions when she swallows, all food is immediately disgorged with much weeping and effluent. She is in a constant state of high fever and is, as we have recently observed, hallucinating.

FERDINAND: But she did see him! She did see Our Saviour!!

ARDILLES: She is losing both her hair and her body mass whilst a tumour the size of a grapefruit is growing in her abdomen. She will evidently be receiving the finest medical assistance available but, Your Majesty, I fear that you must ready yourself to govern the Empire alone.

FERDINAND: Alone?

ARDILLES: Alone.

A silence.

FERDINAND: Dying?

ARDILLES: And I think you must convince her of this unfortunate fact so that she may confess all and be ready to meet the Lord.

FERDINAND: How long will it…

ARDILLES: A week. A month at the most.

FERDINAND: But we are about to wage war on the Muslims!

ARDILLES: Yes.

FERDINAND: We have problems with France!

ARDILLES: Yes.

FERDINAND: And the new world in the west!

ARDILLES: I realise this but it does not alter the...

ISABELLA moans terribly.

FERDINAND: How can God allow such suffering?

ARDILLES: That is a question for the priests, your Majesty.

FERDINAND: And to the devout, to the vigorously devout! This is absurd!

ARDILLES: I really think you must tell her.

ISABELLA vomits terribly.

A long, long silence.

ARDILLES wipes her mouth.

ISABELLA: Tell her what?

FERDINAND: Tell her that...tell her that...

ISABELLA: What, man? What?!

FERDINAND: Our generals in the East are...are low on resources. We...we cannot maintain the supply. The further they advance the more dangerous their situation becomes. We need...well...money.

ISABELLA: Christopher will bring us gold.

FERDINAND: But so far...

ISABELLA: It has been disappointing, I agree.

FERDINAND: We have placed a great deal of our nation's assets ...

ISABELLA: He will deliver.

FERDINAND: But last time he brought back only Indians and most of them were decomposing!

ISABELLA: Forget the past and think only of the present.

FERDINAND: We have investors who are decidedly...

ISABELLA: He will deliver.

FERDINAND: We must welcome back the...

ISABELLA: Nonsense! Never!

FERDINAND: With the Jews' money we can tear down the last mosque, annihilate Islam and then...

ISABELLA: God does not want me compromising with our attitude here. You will notice that the harsher we are with the Jew then the more loudly our own people hail us in the streets.

ISABELLA vomits copiously.

ARDILLES wipes her mouth.

A long silence.

I dreamed of Juana. I think she is mad.

FERDINAND: A little eccentric possibly.

ISABELLA: She must be cured. For the sake of the unity of...

FERDINAND: But she is happy. She is...in love.

ISABELLA: What would she know about that?

FERDINAND: (*Nervously.*) She...she wrote to me.

A silence.

ISABELLA: She writes to you?

FERDINAND: Yes.

ISABELLA: But not to me?

FERDINAND: (*After a pause.*) No.

ISABELLA: And why do you not show…

FERDINAND: She asks me…

ISABELLA: To leave her mother out of it?

FERDINAND: (*After a pause.*) Yes.

ISABELLA: She is an ungrateful child. (*She breaks.*) Oh, she knows how to wound, that girl. She knows how to wound.

FERDINAND: I think she feels she is a disappoint…

ISABELLA: She will soon learn the pain and anguish that accompany parenthood.

FERDINAND: She loves Philip, she says, but…

ISABELLA: She is concerned only with herself and with her own contentment. She thinks nothing of the grand design for which she, for which all of us, were born: the unification of this state. I have been a wandering queen, travelling incessantly around my realm. For decades now I have been waving my waves, smiling my smiles and collecting my taxes. (*Coughs violently.*) There was unrest. And I know the importance of a sovereign's physical presence among her people. So I have birthed my squirming pups in different regions of this land. Like a wild cat pissing on a bush to marks its territory, I have heaved out unwanted daughters in Valladolid, in Seville, in Toledo. I have been torn asunder by these wretched female infants in every corner of Spain. And I have overcome my disappointment at rarely seeing a scrotum hanging there between those fleshy, blood-stained legs. And yet this nation now thinks and acts as one. Every labourer in the field, every monk in his cell, every shipbuilder, every intellectual, every soldier, every priest. Yes, I think only of Spain. Juana thinks only of Juana.

She vomits.

ARDILLES wipes.

I feel weak.

ARDILLES: Then rest.

ISABELLA: I must travel to the Low Countries and visit my child, my future... oh, the Empire...And Rome... Rome... But the Jews are...the Jews are... Where is Ludo?...We must release Ludo...I miss him... Bring me my Ludo...

ARDILLES: Ludo?

FERDINAND: A former servant of ours, imprisoned on the orders of Juana.

ISABELLA: We must release my Ludo. Release my... Makes me laugh, he...

ARDILLES: You must find the right time to tell her.

ISABELLA: Ludo...he makes me laugh, makes me laugh. I want to laugh. (*She sleeps.*)

FERDINAND: I think there is still hope that she will recover. Why must we take your word for it?

ARDILLES: I am a man of science. I work only with the facts.

FERDINAND seems moved.

Your Majesty?

FERDINAND: I really...I love...I have grown to...to love this woman.

ARDILLES: (*After a pause.*) Yes.

FERDINAND: Why did you hesitate?

ARDILLES: Did I hesitate?

FERDINAND: You did. You think I am feigning this emotion? You think of my reputation?

ARDILLES: It is not for me to…

FERDINAND: A man may have mistresses and still love his wife!

ARDILLES: Of course.

FERDINAND: Do *you* love your wife?

ARDILLES: I tolerate her.

FERDINAND: Then do you have lovers?

ARDILLES: I spend a large proportion of my salary on prostitutes. I like coloureds particularly.

FERDINAND: The absence of love in a marriage, Ardilles, is the greatest tragedy in this life.

ARDILLES: I agree, Majesty.

FERDINAND: Ah, a curse upon this existence! A curse upon its perfidious routine!

ARDILLES: Habit is the ballast which chains the dog to its vomit.

FERDINAND: But I cannot believe she is dying. She will die a saint.

ARDILLES: Well…yes.

FERDINAND: She has served the Church. Every breath she has taken has been in its service.

FERDINAND breaks again.

ARDILLES: Your Majesty, I think I must now leave you

with your despair.

FERDINAND suddenly and savagely grabs ARDILLES.

FERDINAND: You think these are not real tears, man! Do
you? You think I weep for effect!? That I feel nothing
for this woman here and that I simulate this misery?

ARDILLES: I think I should go now.

FERDINAND: (*Still holding him roughly.*) I do not want to
be alone!! Oh, the loneliness of my remaining years!!

ARDILLES: We must all confront...

FERDINAND: Do not talk to me of 'we must all'! I am the
fucking king!

ARDILLES: Majesty.

FERDINAND: Perhaps...perhaps I have been a poor
husband! I have lived my life in a carnival of flesh, of
probing tongues and slapping bellies. But how I love
to crush a young pair of breasts beneath my palms, to
slowly unwrap some slut for the very first time! Yes, I
have drunk the juices of a thousand women and shed
the blood of a thousand men. I have used the position
to which I was born to luxuriate in my liking for cunt
and for killing. But now, Ardilles...I see I must change.
I shall devote what's left of my life to the welfare of
my wife. I shall from this moment onwards sleep by
her side, stroking her hair and dabbing her forehead.
I shall swill out her sick bucket, I shall wash her sheets
by hand, I shall take pleasure in wiping the shit and
the piss from her shaking body. She shall not suffer
alone, Ardilles! She shall not suffer alone. (*He throws
ARDILLES down.*) How little we think of our endings,
as we frantically clamber clear of our unfortunate
beginnings. But now here I am, doctor, suddenly grown
quite old. Oh, but what loving hand will wipe my arse
for me when I am dying?! Who will care to wipe my

arse for me?! (*He sinks to his knees.*)

Scene 2

ANGELINA, beside a crib, is reading a letter.

LUDO'S VOICE: Forgive the brevity of this note, my sister, for I must write quickly. There is a guard here who believes that I am a sage of some kind and who, in return for my 'words of wisdom' as he calls them, is prepared to assist me. He brings me the occasional leg of chicken and has also agreed to smuggle out this letter. As you may imagine conditions here are appalling and I confess I do long for death but I am not so unhappy. I see the futility of hatred and am now at peace with this solitary life and the terrible injustice and cruelty of this world. I beg your forgiveness for my attitude towards you and hope that you will also forgive me for the crime I committed against your mistress. Know that it is my love for you which has, sometimes reluctantly, kept me alive all this time. Sister, you will not hear from me again. I wish you a long life and much happiness.

JUANA: (*Entering, heavily pregnant.*) Angelina, Angelina! My Philip is home!

ANGELINA: (*In shock.*) You promised to release him.

JUANA: Did you not hear what I said?

ANGELINA: You have made a fool out of me.

JUANA: Oh, you are so sullen of late. All I ask is that you at least pretend to be excited for me!

ANGELINA: You have betrayed me, my lady.

JUANA: I think that only reasonable.

ANGELINA: (*Taking her swaddled baby from the crib.*) And this boy, this child which I have so recently birthed, he has the pigment of the oppressor.

JUANA: It is the way the wheels of life are oiled. And though I do not ask you to share in the joy I feel at my Philip's impending return, I would hope that your long face could brighten a little and not dampen my mood so.

ANGELINA: God has punished me.

JUANA: Oh, what time is it? All these long, dreary months I have been waiting for this.

ANGELINA: For the crime that was his conception.

JUANA: When he left for the war the little emperor bubbling inside me was scarcely showing, my belly was as flat as the fens themselves, but now...

ANGELINA: How could an infant with this pasty colour sprout from my womb?

JUANA: What time is it? He will be here any moment!

ANGELINA: His flesh, his whole features are those of his...of his...

JUANA: Yes, do smile and try to be just a little happy for me! Now, how do I look?

ANGELINA: How cursed, how damned are the naïve of spirit.

JUANA: I have always thought expectant women quite ridiculous, haven't you? Radiant and glowing, of course, but also somewhat stupidly arrogant. With that untroubled, serene and unthinkingly optimistic look about them. But now that I count myself among their ranks I...

ANGELINA: Like cows chewing the cud.

JUANA: Yes. Rather like cows.

ANGELINA: The world might be blowing itself to hell all around you but just as long as it is kicking...

JUANA: Oh and the little emperor really is! Feel him!

JUANA goes to ANGELINA and places her hand on her belly.

And you have your own life now. Your well-ordered little house. Your daily work, your regular hours. Ordinary citizens, I am told, build their worlds around such certainties. I chose that house for you with great care. The stove, the hearth, the prints on the walls, the drapes around the windows. Yes, such a well-ordered house. I thought you'd be...happy. The views, the bustling square, the lively harbour, the Saturday market close by. Waking to the sound of the gulls, Angelina. Confess...we have come through it all together.

ANGELINA: Will you not even look at my child?

JUANA: But we are friends. You and I.

ANGELINA: How easily you close your eyes and your ears to uncomfortable truths...

JUANA: You snarl like your brother used to snarl, Angelina. I do prefer your company now, I have to admit. Now that you are not moved to agree all the time. Now that I see a little of your spite seeping out. Oh, but you who have never loved will never know the depths of my feelings for my beloved husband!

PHILIP: (*Entering, in army uniform.*) And you will never know the depths of my feelings for you, my love.

JUANA screams with delight and rushes towards PHILIP. She embraces him.

He is weak with fever.

JUANA: My husband! You are safe! I cannot believe it! Let me kiss you.

She covers his face with kisses.

Oh, but you have changed. Your face. You have been wounded. Sit down and tell me about it.

PHILIP: (*Sitting.*) It is too horrible for your ears.

JUANA: Angelina, a drink for my husband, please.

ANGELINA puts the baby back in the crib and pours out a goblet of ale.

You are home now. You can rest. I will take care of you. Your troubles are over.

She takes his sword, which is covered with blood and proceeds to wipe it clean over the following:

PHILIP: These Musselmen, these wailing Alis, these moaning Mustafas, they…

JUANA: Quickly with the ale, please…

PHILIP: (*Drinking.*) They welcome their own annihilation with such joy.

JUANA: (*Touching her belly.*) Philip, what do you think of our little…?

PHILIP: After a battle, there rose against the darkening sky a mass of men. Moaning men, slowly crawling over each other, bellies burst open, entrails sliding down this heap of writhing bodies like so much rope…men, both Christian and Muslim, drowning in each other's blood, mangled arms, severed legs, heads burned and blistered strewn over the sand. One of our men was crucified upon the wheels of his cart. I have seen so much!

JUANA: Philip? Do you see a change in *me* at all?

PHILIP: And yet I shall have to go back…

He bursts into tears and she comforts him as he weeps like a wronged child.

We rode through a village, we slaughtered everybody we could find. I had no choice but to order it! We torched the huts! Then, from nowhere, a flock of them, screeching and clucking like so much demented poultry, came charging down a hill towards us. There were hundreds, and all either flaccid-bellied women clutching their spawn or children with hate-fuelled faces. They ran at us screaming. So I lined up the men and with cannons and crossbows, we massacred them in minutes. Just one girl reached our position, she ran up to me as I was reloading and leapt at me. Oh, the blind rage in her beautiful brown eyes! She lacerated my face with a jagged rock. And as I pushed her away she sank her teeth into my finger. (*Holding up a bandaged finger.*) Look, Juana, I shall never again win an archery competition! In a rage I flipped her on her back, where she wriggled in the dust, gobbing her infidel spit at me. So, from point-blank range, I slammed my axe down into her twelve-year-old mouth, cutting her up in the middle of a curse. Oh God…that I should witness such things!

JUANA: (*Hand over her mouth.*) I do not know what to say.

PHILIP: (*Suddenly recovered.*) Her head burst apart like it was a water melon.

JUANA: Philip? Are you not going to ask after the little emperor here?

PHILIP: I'm so pleased to be home. Out of the fire. I am not worthy.

JUANA: You are babbling. Jabbering. You have a fever. You're speaking in tongues and you…

PHILIP: Many men dropped with the fever, yes. Yellow skin, black and red blotches. Bowels bubbled bleeding from backsides in blue-grey streams. More die from fever! Yes!

JUANA: (*To ANGELINA.*) Angelina, prepare your master's bed.

PHILIP: But no more of that horrible heat, I beg you! No more of that evil, evil heat! I am of Viking stock! Not designed to swelter under a blistering sun. I like hot drinks at night, changing seasons, the wearing of heavy woollen cloaks. Who is this?

JUANA: This is my lady in waiting. She has worked with us for many...

PHILIP: I have trodden the turbaned, fly-riddled heads of your brothers into the dirt! Tell me you don't hate me.

JUANA: She doesn't...

PHILIP: She can speak for herself, surely! She looks at me with disgust. Why is her face so hard? So contemptuous? Come, let me look at you!

ANGELINA approaches him.

I don't like the sneer, Juana. Don't like this lip slightly curling. You are haughty, girl. Haughty and indignant. You have an attitude towards me.

JUANA: She has no attitude.

PHILIP: But you will find that I am a considerate master. Any chance of some pie?

JUANA: Let us talk rather of our joy which even now...

PHILIP: And how I hanker also for mouthfuls of tart!

JUANA: (*With a flourish.*) I now present him to his father.

PHILIP: (*To ANGELINA.*) Tell me, do you have money of your own?

JUANA: She has a small, well-ordered house by the

harbour and I…

PHILIP: (*Slapping his thigh.*) Against all my instincts I find
her attractive! You have been raised as a Christian?
Juana, I feel so unwell.

JUANA: Then rest!

PHILIP: She has a certain quiet dignity about her.
A disdain which rather fires my blood. A man cannot
resist a woman, even a low-born one, who dares to
disdain him!

JUANA: You are offending and embarrassing me!

PHILIP: Do you also disdain money, possessions, security?

ANGELINA: Money is now my God.

PHILIP: I like this woman! She has a deep, earthy voice
which, along with her disdainful sneer, likewise fires the
blood of princes!

JUANA: Did you hear me?

PHILIP: (*To JUANA.*) Fetch me my books!

JUANA: Philip, you need to sleep. You are delirious.

PHILIP: My books, I say!

JUANA: But…

PHILIP: Do remember that you are my wife and as such
you must obey my commands.

JUANA gives him an angry look and then exits.

Females in pod, how they waddle and rock. I have
to say that there is something I cannot countenance
about women who are heavy with child. Friends of
mine would simply take by force a woman they find as
appealing as I find you but that…that is so…uncivilised.
Have we met before? You look down your nose at

92

me. It is rather equine that look of yours. Slightly
regal. I need a little pie! Is that too much to ask for a
conquering hero!? May I confide in you? A soldier away
from his woman and surrounded by barbarity descends
little by little to the state of a beast. It is accepted. I used
whores on a daily basis and was even tempted, as others
are, to take a pretty young boy from the line, but now…
this sickness of mine…I confess it is a disease caught
from a gap-toothed girl in some desolate shack. I think I
might expire from it. And Juana I cannot touch until the
fungus is cleared. She has such high expectations. Oh, I
think I shall die for a crust of pastry!

JUANA returns with an armful of books.

JUANA: Your books.

PHILIP: (*He takes them.*) My books, my books!

JUANA: Philip, you are quite pale. You evidently have a
fever.

PHILIP: (*To ANGELINA.*) Tell me…what do you think of
the German Dominicans?

ANGELINA: I know nothing of them.

PHILIP: These volumes here are highly prized. I inherited
them from some scholarly cousin. Shamefully I have
been using them as door stops. I suspect each of them is
worth more than two years of your wages. Now, this by
Eckhart. A good read, Juana?

JUANA: I will fetch a doctor!

PHILIP: My German is so scandalously poor. They put the
verbs at the end, you know! Now, woman, what does he
say!

JUANA: (*With a suppressed rage.*) Along with the works of
Tauler and Suso, Eckhart encourages the closest possible
intimacy with God attainable in the present life.

PHILIP: Fascinating. (*To ANGELINA.*) Remove the shoes and the book is yours!

JUANA: For the love of God!

PHILIP: (*To ANGELINA.*) Remove the shoes and the book is yours!

ANGELINA does not move.

JUANA: Philip, I have been waiting for your return for all this time! Night after night I have dreamed of nothing but having you in my arms, desiring your touch and your... conversation. The days have been long and the evenings almost unendurable. I have been sick with anxiety, at the thought of you being cut down in battle and that I might never see you again. There are marks on the wall by our bed where I have been counting down the days like a child, waiting for her festival gift. Please...I beg you...do not humiliate me in front of my...

ANGELINA slowly steps out of her shoes. She takes the book from PHILIP.

PHILIP: And this by John Herold? Would fetch a pretty price on the market, this! What does he say? (*No answer.*) What does he say, woman?! What does he say?

JUANA: (*With a suppressed rage.*) In this book Herold encourages his readers to strive for goals which are attainable by all souls and refutes the elitist musings of the mystics.

PHILIP: (*To ANGELINA.*) Fascinating. Remove that and the book is yours.

ANGELINA slowly removes an article of clothing. She takes the book from PHILIP.

And this by von Weida? Quickly!

JUANA: (*With a suppressed rage.*) Mark von Weida insists that the faithful be satisfied with a practical sort of spirituality and desist from mystical aspirations.

PHILIP: (*To ANGELINA.*) Fascinating. Remove that and the book is yours!

ANGELINA slowly removes an article of clothing. She takes the book from PHILIP.

And finally, the jewel in the crown: this by John Nider.

He looks to his wife again.

JUANA: John Nider and his contemporaries speak of man in concrete situations and direct their teaching and preaching to morality and the care of souls.

ANGELINA slowly removes her final article of clothing. She takes the volume from PHILIP and stands naked before him, clutching the books.

PHILIP: You are now a wealthy woman.

JUANA: Angelina, please! Put your clothing back on!

PHILIP rises and walks unsteadily around the naked woman.

PHILIP: She is like a goddess, is she not! A statue of some exotic goddess, carved from the rarest ebony!

JUANA: Angelina, take your books and your clothes and then go!!

PHILIP: Yes, go and retire somewhere beautiful!

ANGELINA gathers her clothing and with a slow dignity exits with her books.

JUANA stifles a sob. She runs out.

(*Looking round, calling off.*) Look, is anyone going to bring me that crust of pie!?

The baby begins to cry behind him.

PHILIP, puzzled, is stopped in his tracks. He looks around.

Scene 3

A dungeon. LUDO, a beatific smile on his face, hangs in chains from the wall. DE LA CRUZ is sweeping the floor.

DE LA CRUZ: So, boss, tell me 'bout sufferin'.

LUDO: (*With patience.*) Man suffers because there is no other way for him to mature. There is no other way for him to grow.

DE LA CRUZ: Right?

LUDO: Man suffers because only through suffering can he become more aware. And this is the key to it all: awareness, the awareness of self and following on from that the awareness of others...

DE LA CRUZ: And that's, what, compassion?

LUDO: Compassion. Yes.

DE LA CRUZ: I 'ate my life. It irks me. And I 'ate those whom life does not irk. Those for whom life is a source of constant delight, these I 'ate the most.

LUDO: (*Inhaling deeply.*) I concentrate on the breath.

DE LA CRUZ: Fink of me, when I leave you 'ere tonight, boss. Back to the wife. Back to the screamin' gannets. Fink of me tonight as you 'ang 'ere worry free. (*Pause.*) I drink.

LUDO: You...?

DE LA CRUZ: I drink. I have a problem with drink. I 'ave tried see, since we started our little chats, to treat her a bit...well...better.

LUDO: The happier she is, the happier you will be. I assure you.

DE LA CRUZ: But she's got this mouf on 'er. She don't like me drinkin', boss. Says I get nasty. Says I get 'andy with me fists, boss.

LUDO: And do you?

DE LA CRUZ: Not always with me fists, boss. Caught her a vicious blow in the face with a saucepan. Last week, this was. Fursday dinner time. She served up offal again.

LUDO: And she…?

DE LA CRUZ: Out like a light till the followin' mornin'. The kids gave me such disrespectful looks, they did. I 'ate offal. (*Throws the broom in a rage.*) Why did I marry?

LUDO: Socrates said: 'One must get married. If you get a good wife you will be happy, and if you get a wife like mine you will become a philosopher. Either way you will have profited.'

DE LA CRUZ: His missus 'ad a mouf, did she?

LUDO: And a most violent temper.

DE LA CRUZ: Sounds familiar.

LUDO: Yet I think it is better for the truthseeker to avoid women altogether. A woman will not care to share you with the truth. A woman is always a mystery to…

DE LA CRUZ: I don't care 'bout the troof. I just want some fuckin' peace! (*He picks up the broom and starts sweeping.*)
I 'ate my life. It irks me.

LUDO: I'm sorry.

DE LA CRUZ: I wake up in the mornin's and I'm irked. I munch at me breakfast and I'm irked. All I got to look forward to is being irked down 'ere all day, the sun shinin' outside, the sky a pleasin' blue and me irked down 'ere all day. I walk down the street from the 'ouse and I'm irked. Meet the same people, outside the same shops, raisin' the same tired eyebrows, and I'm walking past the same buildin's, the same trees. And I'm just irked. I yawn frough my life like a sleepwalker and I got no loot. She says I spend all our wedge on drink. Says I piss it all against the wall.

LUDO: And do you?

DE LA CRUZ: A man must take his pleasures when he can. (*Pause.*) And then I leave 'ere after twelve hours of it and I'm into the pub. Irked again. I'm sat at the same stool and I'm with the same people. And we all say the same fings. Same fings over and over. Every night the same. And then I'm back to the 'ouse and then 'er with the mouf, well she's at me again. We fight, the little ones cry, 'specially the girl, I give the wife some of the old in-and-out and then it's kip time again. Then it's up with the lark for yet more of the same.

LUDO: You must take consolation where you…

DE LA CRUZ: Ah, fuck it! I 'ate my life. It irks me.

LUDO: Yes.

DE LA CRUZ: Wouldn't mind but I got no loot. You work like a cunt and you got no loot. No loot to call your own, boss. Ah, fuck it. I 'ate my life. It irks me.

LUDO: Jesus said, 'Blessed be the solitary and the elect' and by this I think he means that…

DE LA CRUZ: I know others who are irked an'all and there's a lot of us out there. In these jobs. What mind the gaols and put out the fires and sweep the fuckin' roads, there's a lot of us out there and the anger is risin'. The anger is risin' like heat from the street. Let it come down, I tell ya. Let it all come down. I 'ate my life. It irks me.

FERDINAND: (*Entering, hand over his mouth.*) Oh, my God!

LUDO: It is the King!

FERDINAND: The stench. It's repulsive.

DE LA CRUZ: The King!

FERDINAND: Ah, there you are.

DE LA CRUZ: (*Sinking to his knees.*) Your Majesty!!??

FERDINAND: So this is the rancid little hole in which you have been mouldering away, is it?

DE LA CRUZ: (*With a more refined accent.*) Your Majesty, this is a most unexpected...

FERDINAND: I crush the bones of rats beneath my feet and slip in faecal matter.

DE LA CRUZ: If I had known you were coming, sir, then...

FERDINAND: It's churning my bowels and it's turning my stomach.

DE LA CRUZ: If you would permit me, Your Majesty, to offer you just a small token of my esteem by way of a drink?

FERDINAND: Make it a strong one.

DE LA CRUZ: Words alone cannot express the great honour you do me in...

FERDINAND: What is it?

DE LA CRUZ: A gooseberry liqueur.

FERDINAND: Fuck that, man! I need something decent to swig!

DE LA CRUZ: I remain, sir, your very humble servant. (*Goes to exits. Stops. Aside.*) Wait till I tell the missus 'bout this, the cunt!

FERDINAND: So…here you stink?

LUDO: Yes.

FERDINAND: And fester?

LUDO: I concentrate on the breath.

FERDINAND: Meaning?

LUDO: Life for me has become an exercise in meditation. My only occupations are the occasional flight of imagination or memory and the rising and falling of the ribcage.

FERDINAND: You don't get bored?

LUDO: Surprisingly not. My inhalations and exhalations are like the eternal and comforting sound of waves crashing against a shore.

FERDINAND: I hate my life. It irks me.

LUDO: You swing your suffering over your head like a cudgel.

FERDINAND: Yes, and somebody must be beaten with it. (*Pause.*) I miss you actually. Miss our little…routines.

LUDO: Yes.

FERDINAND: You happy to die down here then?

LUDO: There is nowhere I would rather be. I am free from the world and therefore closer to God.

FERDINAND: Death holds no horror for you?

LUDO: (*After a pause.*) No.

FERDINAND: I hate my life. It irks me. (*Pause.*) The

Queen wants to see you.

LUDO: She does?

FERDINAND: She says that you…make her laugh. She wants to release you. She wants you to be her… entertainment. What do you have to say about that?

LUDO: I am resigned to this isolated death. I am resigned to never seeing the light of day again. My loose ends have been…

FERDINAND: I told her that if you were still amusing, then I would order your immediate release but that if all this incarceration had dulled your sense of humour, that here you must remain. Atmosphere at court is all doom and gloom these days. We need someone capable of organising a little…sing-song.

LUDO: And this master of ceremonies is me?

FERDINAND: That remains to be seen.

LUDO: My life is over.

FERDINAND: You would rather die down here than be a jester to kings?

LUDO: I would rather die.

FERDINAND: Let us test this fearlessness in the face of death, shall we?

FERDINAND suddenly and savagely holds a sword to LUDO's throat.

I know the designs you have had on my women, my daughters and my wife…I know you with your youth and your pride and your fine young muscular body. Yes, I have been jealous. I am scared of you people! Women want you! They want you but they fear you! You fine, fine man!! And we are scared yes that you may all rise up in rebellion against us! Take back what we have stolen! This I shall confess. But, now I am going to end your life and you will leave not a trace behind. You will die alone and unloved and forgotten just as I shall die alone and...

LUDO: Please!

FERDINAND: So this is not the way you want to go then? You want to drift into a benign old age before God quietly summons you?

LUDO: Please!

FERDINAND: You have a matter of seconds in which to make me laugh! Sing a song, tell a joke, juggle or dance. But ensure you play the clown, man or your days are done!

A silence.

I can smell the terror on your sweat. There is a terrible fear in your eyes.

A silence.

You have made your choice, slave, and now your days of choices are over.

FERDINAND makes ready to kill LUDO.

LUDO: (*In desperation.*) Your Majesty, I beg you. I am still a young man. Spare me! I would like to see again the vast ocean from a clifftop, make love to a young and beautiful woman, turn my face to the sun and the world is vast and there is wine and song and... And there is so much still to learn. Still so much to learn and to experience! I beg you, Majesty!

FERDINAND: Then amuse me!

LUDO suddenly adopts the exaggerated vocal and physical characteristics of a preacher. This is the black man mocking himself in order to please his white master.

LUDO: 'Weeeellll, in de beginning God created de heavens and de earth! Now de earth was formless and empty, darkness was over de surface of de deep, and de Spirit of God was hovering over de waters.'

FERDINAND begins to laugh. It builds.

'And den God said, "Let dere be light", and dere was light. God saw that de light was good, and he separated de light from de darkness. God called de light de "day", and de darkness he called de "night". And dere was evening, and dere was morning: de first day.' And den God in his wisdom he…

FERDINAND, buckled over, drops the sword.

FERDINAND: (*Breathless from laughter.*) Oh, that's really good. That really is good. That really is very, very funny.

DE LA CRUZ comes on with two goblets of wine.

That really is most amusing. I am even wiping away a tear, look.

DE LA CRUZ: A drink, your Majesty. (*Aside.*) Wait till I tell the missus 'bout this, the cunt!

FERDINAND: You can shove your golden goblets up your arse, gaoler, and then you can release this man. Clean him up and then bring him to court. Be sure to dress him as a fool. He really is very entertaining. And entertainment is…it is precisely what the king and queen currently require!

FERDINAND exits.

DE LA CRUZ stares after him, devastated. Then he drinks, hurls the goblets down and turns to LUDO in a rage. He spits at LUDO then runs off.

Scene 4

ANGELINA pursued by PHILIP, with an armful of books. The crib.

ANGELINA: You must be patient.

PHILIP: But you are torturing me. One last time in your arms, I beg you!

ANGELINA: I want the whole library.

PHILIP: But it is worth a fortune. My family have invested almost all their wealth…

ANGELINA: Then you shall never taste me again.

PHILIP: But I must, I must.

JUANA screams in agony off.

ANGELINA: Your wife even now is about to suffer the torments of creating new life. Your little emperor is burrowing through her bones as we speak.

PHILIP: Oh, but I simply cannot abide these…these grizzling shitters.

ANGELINA: Even though it may one day rule over Europe?

PHILIP: It is you that I want. The sweet-smelling skin, the slim waist, the curve of your hips, your wild, indignant face.

ANGELINA: Later.

PHILIP: And those wonderful lips.

ANGELINA: Do not touch me!

PHILIP: God, I ache for you.

ANGELINA: Then you shall have me once more, sweet prince.

PHILIP: Please...even the words are enough to... I am in agony down here so hard does it strain at my breeches.

ANGELINA: I need more money.

PHILIP: I will give you all that I have.

JUANA screams in agony off.

ANGELINA: Then listen: at the next full moon, you must come to my house.

PHILIP: That well-ordered house.

ANGELINA: The views, the bustling square.

PHILIP: The lively harbour.

ANGELINA: The Saturday market close by.

PHILIP: I shall be there.

ANGELINA: And then, provided you bring with you the Aquinas I require...

PHILIP: But you will ruin me...

ANGELINA: *The Treatise on the Truth of the Catholic Faith, against Unbelievers.*

PHILIP: That volume alone is worth more money than...

ANGELINA: Only then shall you have what you desire.

A final scream of agony from JUANA.

Now, go.

PHILIP: You witch, you...assassin.

PHILIP leaves.

In despair JUANA rushes on, holding up her swaddled baby.

JUANA: This infant is mulatto! This infant is mulatto!

ANGELINA: Mulatto?

JUANA: Mulatto! Mulatto!

ANGELINA: The infant is…mulatto?

JUANA: This infant is mulatto! This infant is mulatto!

ANGELINA: I…congratulate you.

JUANA: Congratulate me?

ANGELINA: Yes.

JUANA: Why are you smiling? You are laughing at me!

ANGELINA: I am discovering a little…happiness.

JUANA: You talk to me of happiness! The infant is mulatto! The infant is mulatto!

ANGELINA: Mu…lat…to…

JUANA: Can you not see that this is my ruin?! You and the memory of you will disappear as soon as the first maggot is hatched in your putrefying body, your whole existence will be like a light footprint in the sand, washed away by the force of a single wave…but my name, my name, my story will be written down in history books! This is a catastrophe!

JUANA hands the baby to ANGELINA.

ANGELINA stares at the baby and becomes transfixed.

Can you not see? The infant is mulatto! The infant is…

ANGELINA: (*Suddenly transported with delight.*) My mother! My mother's face now stares up at me! It has been decades since I saw this face. This is my mother's face. You are alive. They chopped you into scraps before my eyes but now you are alive again. You breathe.

Your stare is the same as on that day. You are shocked,
bewildered. Frightened. My mother. (*Turning to JUANA.*)
This is my mother. I cannot believe the evidence of
my...

JUANA: I am undone! I am undone! The world has gone
mad! Mad! Mad! Mad!

ANGELINA: You have come back to me. Oh, this is
indeed a happy day!

JUANA: What am I to do? I have produced not only a
female but also a mulatto! My husband will be here
shortly and I shall be beheaded as a traitor... (*Down on
her knees.*) Oh, dear God in heaven...I beg you to save
me. I am not ready to die. I know I am unworthy of
your love and your assistance but I implore you to show
me how I may save myself . Alfonso, I...

The other baby – in the crib – cries out.

*JUANA looks up from her prayer. She slowly walks to the
crib. She looks at the baby for the first time.*

A long silence.

Philip...?

ANGELINA: Mother...

JUANA: My God...my God...this is my Philip in this
crib...

ANGELINA: You are my mother. My dear, beloved
mother...

*JUANA takes the baby from the crib. She walks back to
ANGELINA.*

JUANA: Angelina?

ANGELINA turns.

God has blessed us both this day.

ANGELINA: God...has...blessed...us...both.

JUANA: I think we...understand each other.

ANGELINA: Oh, my mother. I can see you have been cast back into this inferno against your will. The apprehension in your stare.

JUANA: I think that we do.

ALFONSO appears on his cross. He laughs.

ALFONSO: How quickly one crime leads to another.

JUANA: Go away!

ALFONSO: But you called for me.

JUANA: Not now, not now!

ALFONSO: Your instinct for self-preservation is accumulating victims, Juana.

JUANA: The state must have its future.

ALFONSO: Yet it seems that this is the way of the world.

JUANA: And the future must be white.

ALFONSO: Put the baby back. It is not yours.

JUANA: Leave!

ALFONSO: Do as I say.

JUANA: What do you care?

ANGELINA: (*To her baby.*) I understand you completely.

JUANA: You do not exist! You are a spirit in my brain!

ANGELINA: Your destiny is set and your choices are few.

ALFONSO: Give me the child.

ALFONSO gets down from the cross.

ANGELINA: Yet this is your choice.

ALFONSO: Give him to me.

JUANA: No! This is the little emperor!

ANGELINA: Your only choice.

ALFONSO: And your are not fit to be his mother!

JUANA: I *am* his mother!

ANGELINA: A short and brutal life of scouring pans, dusting furniture, your back breaking, your fingers bleeding. Forever evicted even in the land of your birth. Or parting your legs for pot-bellied businessmen. Death down an alleyway. Diseases in the dark.

ALFONSO: (*Approaching her.*) Give him to me. You are unwell...

JUANA: (*Producing a knife.*) I have a blade, see!

ANGELINA: Yes, I understand you completely. You smile up your gratitude. You smile.

ALFONSO: You have been cutting your forearms again...

JUANA: Get back on your cross!

ANGELINA: Then ready yourself.

ALFONSO: Give me the baby...

JUANA: Get away, get away, get away!!

ALFONSO: This is madness, Juana. Madness.

JUANA: Do not say it! Do not say that word again!

JUANA stabs ALFONSO, who drops like a stone, writhing. After a time he is still.

A long silence.

So…rise again.

ALFONSO does not move.

Rise, I command you…

ALFONSO does not move.

So now…now I shall have no-one to depend on but myself.

She rushes off with the baby.

ANGELINA: Yours has been a brief glimpse. But a brief glimpse is all you have needed. You have seen your god and now you may go. Yes, go home then, my mother. Go home, my people, and be still.

ANGELINA slowly throttles the baby.

When the act is over she slowly looks up. She closes her eyes, at peace.

Scene 5

Music. The Royal Celebration. To huge applause and cheering, JUANA and PHILIP dance in the court to celebrate the birth of their child. It is both graceful and touching and is executed with some skill. Lights up on ISABELLA in her bed, with FERDINAND praying beside her. Lights up on LUDO, he is chained and is sobbing. Lights up on ANGELINA as ARDILLES takes her violently from behind. The dance continues.

Scene 6

ANGELINA is hacking meat with a large meat cleaver. The blows fall at regular intervals and become more violent as ANGELINA's madness escalates.

ANGELINA: My brother, hear me! It is I who have condemned you to your life in a cage! Forgive me! I,

with my feeble respect for virtue, have robbed you of
a glorious death and kept you a slave. We were not
born to be captives. Now I must contrive to share just
a little of my pain with those whose beautiful lives
have crushed us. Do we live like worms, grovelling in
the dirt, begging for crumbs or do we die like gods,
magnificent and drunk on courage? And so, my lord
and my lady, I curse this flesh. I curse each mouthful
you will shovel down your gulping throats. I condemn
you to life. To a life without love, to a life of silent
contempt, of unfathomable loneliness and of deep and
endless disappointment, where the more luxury you
accrue the more agony and fear you shall feel. Yes, soon
you shall feast on what you have slaughtered: a little
African flesh. And then you shall suffer like the brutes,
like the well-mannered beasts that you are.

Lights down on her as PHILIP enters.

PHILIP: The sound of your voice! Please. Just leave me
alone!

JUANA follows.

JUANA: Philip, what is happening? I am your wife, your
woman. I need to be touched. I need to be loved.
Without your love I shall shrivel away and die.

PHILIP: I do love you.

JUANA: Without touch, love is just a word.

PHILIP: What is this preoccupation with love? Can you
not accept that I love you and lets have an end to all
this...emotion.

JUANA: An end to emotion!?

PHILIP: You must content yourself with your reading and
your...

JUANA: I want you to fuck me, Philip!

PHILIP: Your language, really…it is not…ladylike.

JUANA: It is not ladylike to say it but, oh, the things you used to want me to do…

PHILIP: I cannot bear the domestic life. I am…restless. I need to be in the world.

JUANA: You *are* in the world. The world is us. Our family.

PHILIP: The family is your world. This is…stifling!

JUANA: No!

PHILIP: There is a chasm between the sexes, Juana. A great unbridgeable chasm.

JUANA: This is not so!

PHILIP: You are interested in the lives of those around you, the local life, I am engaged in what is happening in the New World, in France, in England, the East. I am, as I said, restless. There is in the male this constant lack of ease. It is how it should be. This gives him a need for endless movement. The female however is more at peace with this life. And I cannot be forever sitting, like you, with a book or a piece of embroidery.

JUANA: So I am to be chained by the simple existence of my womb to the sink and to the stove?

PHILIP: You have servants.

JUANA: You have changed.

PHILIP: It was the war. It…

JUANA: Nonsense…nonsense!!

PHILIP: I am fatigued.

JUANA: Not too fatigued to flirt with that hare-lipped

countess from Hanover!!?

PHILIP: She is not hare-lipped, Juana.

JUANA: Not too fatigued to paddle palms with the wife of the Rotterdam mayor?!!

PHILIP: Juana.

JUANA: Not too fatigued to boom out your fake laughter with that big-bosomed Bavarian bitch, or prance with the trollop who has invited you to her 'wonderful' new castle in Kent??!!

PHILIP: I have to be courteous to our guests. And she invited both of us.

JUANA: I decline!!

PHILIP: You are shouting, Juana. You are attracting attention.

JUANA: And the way you stare at Angelina! Always ogling the girl!

PHILIP: (*Laughing.*) It is in your imagination.

JUANA: You are making a fool of me.

PHILIP: I respect nobody like I respect you.

JUANA: At this moment I care nothing for your respect! It is your body that I want!

PHILIP: You are raving. You must calm down.

JUANA: I will not calm down! It is my right!

PHILIP: Do not talk to me of rights!

JUANA: Philip, please. Come to my bed now and…

PHILIP: Don't say it!

JUANA: Do I make you sigh? Oh, my poor dear Philip.

That a stupid little wife must make you sigh so with her unreasonable demands!

PHILIP: You do not understand me.

JUANA: You do not let me try.

PHILIP: Listen…we must both make the best of a bad situation. We were forced upon each other.

JUANA: Yes, but we love!

PHILIP: We must come to an arrangement. We must draw up some form of agreement.

JUANA: We started out as lovers and now you would have us converse as lawyers!

PHILIP: Juana…

JUANA: Don't say it. Don't talk to me like I am some unruly child, who needs the facts of life explained to her. Don't you dare insult me. You, who does not even read!

PHILIP: There is more to life than the turning of pages!

JUANA: There is more to life than eating and drinking!

PHILIP: You see, we are too different.

JUANA: We are not too different. I just never see you! I never see my son. That would be a slight compensation.

PHILIP: He is being groomed for his future role.

JUANA: He is barely a month old!

PHILIP: Juana, you are shouting.

JUANA: That tone of a kindly yet condescending schoolmaster just starting to lose his patience.

PHILIP: The servants snigger behind the curtains!

JUANA: Let them snigger! Let them piss themselves at our unhappiness!

PHILIP: Your language is...

JUANA: My language is my language and you cannot take it from me!

PHILIP: I shall leave now.

JUANA: Don't you dare turn your back on me.

PHILIP: Don't talk to me of what I dare do and dare not do in my own house.

JUANA: This is not your house! You are never in it!

PHILIP: I order you to keep your voice down!

JUANA: Fuck your orders...

PHILIP: The language!!

JUANA: (*Jumping up and wrapping her legs around his waist.*) Fuck me!

PHILIP: (*Trying to shake her off.*) No.

JUANA: Fuck me!!

PHILIP: There are servants...

JUANA: Ram me against the wall! Take from behind! Whatever pleases you, I...

He flings her to the floor. She sprawls. A long silence.

There is sniggering from behind a curtain.

PHILIP: And now the working classes are laughing at us again.

JUANA: I detest the working classes.

PHILIP: Get up!

JUANA: You are becoming, Philip, inordinately fond of using the imperative.

PHILIP: It is what I was born for!!

A sniggering from behind the curtains.

Stop laughing or I will have you all in the Scavenger's Daughter!!

The sniggering stops.

Now, get up.

JUANA: No.

PHILIP: This is intolerable.

He suddenly and angrily grabs hold of JUANA and pulls her violently to her feet.

What is the matter with you?

JUANA hurls herself at PHILIP and kisses him. With all her strength she keeps her mouth on his as he tries to push her off.

Eventually, PHILIP extricates himself from her and, with a single blow, sends her flying across the stage. She crashes to the floor.

The sniggering behind the curtains returns.

JUANA: That was at least passionate.

PHILIP: (*He hands her a handkerchief.*) Your mouth is bleeding.

JUANA: Let it bleed.

PHILIP: Stop laughing!!

The sniggering stops.

JUANA: Philip, why have we become like this? The way we are looking at each other now. Where once there was love…

PHILIP: If I hear that word one more time…

JUANA: Philip, have you been with other women?

No answer.

Shall I assume from your silence that you have?

No answer.

Each moment you are silent a little more of my life leaks away.

PHILIP: (*With difficulty.*) I…am…true.

JUANA: You lie!

PHILIP: I am not like other men.

JUANA: Who is she, who is she? You keep me in this tower night after night and all the while you are between the thighs of another!

PHILIP: I am with my friends, I have told you. I need the company of men.

JUANA: I never see you! I am so…alone!

PHILIP: I prefer the conversation of men. Chit-chat, you understand. Over a draught or two of ale.

LOUTS: (*Off.*) Of ale!!!

JUANA: You are turning me…

PHILIP: I must go, my love. I must go.

JUANA: Mad. Mad. Quite, quite mad.

PHILIP: I beg you…do not make another scene.

PHILIP exits sheepishly.

The sniggers from behind the curtain start up again as JUANA wrestles with her agony.

ANGELINA comes on from the other side.

ANGELINA: There are clearly some who find the agony of others entertaining and yet I am not yet one of these. But to delight in the fall of those who wield power over you is simply human nature. So do not look for sympathy here. But do you really know pain? Is not your pain merely an invention, an indulgence? What right have you, whose every whim is immediately satisfied, who can never know true suffering, what right have you to tear at your hair and cry to the moon? I do not care of course. It is bliss. This not caring. It really is bliss.

JUANA: (*Not looking up.*) Tell them…to stop laughing.

ANGELINA: They need to fill their empty hours.

JUANA: They should not have empty hours.

ANGELINA: The empire prospers. If you want them to work and to die for you, you will need to provide them with something. And human beings must be amused.

JUANA: And he is squandering all our money on pleasure. Our beloved books, my books… Say you will return my priceless books. I cannot live without my…

ANGELINA: Those books are now mine.

JUANA: I feel such…fear.

ANGELINA: You fear for your reputation, for your place in history?

JUANA: Yes.

ANGELINA: You fear aloneness. You are scared of not achieving, never becoming? Of ending your days as… nothing, as no-one?

JUANA: To be no-one…to be nobody…

ANGELINA: The Catholic scheme is hierarchical.
Fabricated by the thoughts of men. It feeds off your
fears, depends upon them.

JUANA: An artificial structure.

ANGELINA: It is a web of illusion.

JUANA: And this foolish fear of fucking!

ANGELINA: End the fear and the system collapses.

JUANA: How do you know so much about all this?

ANGELINA: I have been…reading.

JUANA: I can no longer. My misery, my confusion
prevents me from concentrating on the words. It is now
just so much coloured ink dancing before my eyes!

ANGELINA: It is true that the ideas of others are of little
consolation.

JUANA: And my boy…I never see. They have taken him
away. They are preparing him for his life of brutality
and prayer, his lonely life of slaughtering and self-hatred
and oh, I must fill this ache, this emptiness which gnaws
and which chews.

ANGELINA: But that emptiness is life.

JUANA: I am caving in upon myself. The world drifts
further away from me as each day passes and, oh I had
such an education! I only ever wanted to…participate,
to contribute! (*Pause.*) I believe that Philip loves another.
And I cannot bear the thought of…

ANGELINA: So banish the thought.

JUANA: How can I simply…?

ANGELINA: Your thought is not real. Know that once it is observed, it vanishes. Try.

JUANA closes her eyes, wrestles with her soul for a time. A silence then the sound of passionate lovers. She quickly opens her eyes. The sound stops.

JUANA: Oh, I cannot. In the darkness there was silence for a time but then, from nowhere, this image: light from the candle fluttering, dancing over the bed and the stones of the wall. Two figures entwined in linen. A man, on top, is naked, perspiring, his swinging, swollen scrotum jangling between his thighs, those heaving hairy buttocks pounding, his whole thrusting torso chopping at a harlot's guts. Her bruised and chubby legs pointing to the ceiling, her two flanks flattened, her toes curling, her bangled arms clutching at his clammy neck.

ANGELINA: He is grimacing like a man under torture.

JUANA: His teeth exposed like a hound in the sewer.

ANGELINA: His tongue, like a fish writhing on a hook, flapping at you, gagging in you.

JUANA: His rough stubble scrubbing the delicate flesh…

ANGELINA: His ale-breath upon you!

JUANA: The saliva within you!

ANGELINA: And the spit, and the spit, and the spit!

JUANA: (*With desperation.*) Who *is* she???

ANGELINA: (*After a pause.*) I think I know.

A silence as JUANA struggles with the agony of this discovery.

JUANA: (*Weakly.*) I must have the…truth.

ANGELINA: Then I can help you.

JUANA: Please. Do.

ANGELINA: At the next full moon, the time when the lunatics roam the streets…at the next full moon, after you have dined here you must come to my home. Come to my home and then the truth shall be yours.

ANGELINA leaves.

JUANA chokes back her despair. She then drops to the floor in a faint.

The sniggers from behind the curtain resume.

Scene 7

ISABELLA in her bed. She is closely inspecting a small nugget of gold. COLUMBUS stands by, anxiously.

ISABELLA: Well, Mr Columbus…it is, I agree, decidedly pretty. I knew you wouldn't let us down.

COLUMBUS: (*Nervous laugh.*) No. Well…no… But of course… Absolutely.

ISABELLA: There's a constant supply? Because we need to move quickly.

COLUMBUS: Absolutely.

ISABELLA: (*Coughs.*) Ah, God is testing me. I have been sick for so long.

COLUMBUS: Oh…Well…I'm so sorry…to hear that. Yes.

ISABELLA: It's a frightful bore.

COLUMBUS: Oh… Absolutely yes. (*Nervous laugh.*) Sickness. A bore. Yes. I have seen…on my travels… it's…

ISABELLA: So how will all this gold translate? Once we've paid off the investors. When can we, in your opinion, start to fund our various expansions?

COLUMBUS: Yes. Of course. Absolutely.

ISABELLA: I believe this question required information of some kind. It was not simply seeking an affirmative.

COLUMBUS: No. Absolutely not. Ah…

ISABELLA: Nor a negative.

COLUMBUS: Oh. Absolutely.

ISABELLA: Are you alright, Christopher? You seem…

COLUMBUS: Oh yes, absolutely…

ISABELLA: Edgy.

COLUMBUS: Edgy? Well… I suppose I… ·

ISABELLA: Are you under the weather?

COLUMBUS: Yes…a little. Absolutely. I have been, I suppose…

ISABELLA: They have the plague in England, you know.

COLUMBUS: Yes…yes…

ISABELLA: And the king's boy dead through tuberculosis.

COLUMBUS: Really? That is…sad.

ISABELLA: Fifteen years old.

COLUMBUS: Oh, dear. I am…that is…well…young.

ISABELLA: His wife Elizabeth recently died in childbirth.

COLUMBUS: Oh God. That's so… I'm sorry.

ISABELLA: And to assuage his grief the king now wants to marry my Catherine.

COLUMBUS: Oh, well that's…nice.

ISABELLA: I've said not a chance.

COLUMBUS: No. Absolutely.

ISABELLA: Henry the Seventh is old and infirm and his rule is almost up.

COLUMBUS: Of course it is, of course it is.

She coughs and wheezes horribly.

A silence.

COLUMBUS laughs nervously.

Another silence.

A prolonged and painful moan from ISABELLA.

ISABELLA: He evidently cannot see this cruel fact staring him in the face.

COLUMBUS: Yes, it's clear. It's clear he can't. Abso...

ISABELLA: Why on earth would I want my daughter to live as a widow in England? I want her on the fucking throne! I've said she should marry Henry, the younger, much prettier prince.

COLUMBUS: Oh, good idea. Absolutely.

ISABELLA: Catherine of Aragon and Henry Tudor of England.

COLUMBUS: Absolutely.

ISABELLA: What is wrong, Columbus? You are shaking, man! I'm the one who is ill!

COLUMBUS: Absolutely you are, yes. And I...I...

ISABELLA: Get a hold of yourself.

COLUMBUS: Yes. Of course. That is imperative.

ISABELLA: It is imperative.

COLUMBUS: Imperative. (*Nervous laugh.*) Absolutely.

ISABELLA: Now you were saying...what, in hard currency, does this overall haul amount to?

No answer.

The colour has drained completely from your face.

No answer.

I am now in the grip of a most uneasy feeling.

No answer.

(*Aside.*) And I cannot say it is something which entirely agrees with me.

COLUMBUS: (*Genuflecting, head bowed, speaking rapidly.*) I kneel before you now, Your Majesty, as the most abject and wretched of men. I am guilty before my sovereign and guilty before God. It is possible that in the years to come I will be thought of as a fearless navigator of oceans, a brave explorer, a discoverer of new worlds, a noble entrepreneur. They will no doubt erect huge statues of me in their capital cities. And yet to myself I symbolise the great murderous failure of the capitalist experiment. From the very outset, Majesty, I betrayed my soul. The lifelong pension of ten thousand marevedis you offered to the first man to sight land I falsely claimed for myself. It was in fact the hawk-eyed Rodrigo from his crow's nest who shouted 'land ahoy' that fateful day and yet it is I who am now enjoying the money that is rightfully his. Oh, my soul is in such torment, Majesty! And when the tribesmen waded out to greet us I saw tiny ornaments in their ears and, oh I had such wild visions of golden fields. We took some prisoner, tortured them to know where these fields lay but they did not, could not say! We then plundered the Caribbean islands, taking all women and children for sex and for slavery. We have killed and raped many, so many, Majesty. I have committed so many unspeakable acts! But still no gold, just flakes of ore from the rivers. I set up camps where these people worked and died by the thousands. I would for pleasure sometimes pick the slower ones off with my musket. But still no gold. I have boatloads of naked, miserable Indians but that is all. Oh, my soul is in such torment, Majesty! I am a monster but I shall be one day celebrated as a hero. I beg your forgiveness for I am sick of sin. And it is my sad duty to inform you that what you presently have in your hand is the largest piece of the mineral that we could find.

A long, tense silence as COLUMBUS whimpers.

ISABELLA: For your crimes against humanity you must answer to God but are you seriously telling me that I am to finance my wars of conquest with a mere nugget!!??

FERDINAND and LUDO enter.

LUDO, dressed as a clown, is giving the king a piggyback.

FERDINAND: Canter, damn you! Canter!

LUDO canters.

Now, neigh a little.

LUDO neighs.

And snort, if you please.

LUDO snorts.

FERDINAND: (*To ISABELLA.*) Just like my favourite mare, darling!

ISABELLA: What are you doing?

FERDINAND: We are the entertainment.

ISABELLA: Entertainment?

FERDINAND: We are here to lighten your darkness, temporarily to transport you away from the problems of the age and the endless torments of the human soul.

ISABELLA: I am not in the mood.

FERDINAND: Ludo has been rehearsing all day.

ISABELLA: I thought Ludo was languishing in gaol.

FERDINAND: No longer, darling. He has now been reborn as a pantomime horse.

ISABELLA: Why does he have those bells?

FERDINAND: Because they are amusing.

ISABELLA: Is that really you, Ludo?

LUDO: Yes, Majesty.

ISABELLA: You have lost your self-respect then?

LUDO: Mortality holds more horrors for me than I imagined.

FERDINAND: Indeed! The man seems to prefer life with endless humiliation to the alternative: oblivion with dignity.

ISABELLA coughs and splutters.

We will recover you with a little dumbshow.

ISABELLA: But I like songs!

FERDINAND: We have no songs.

ISABELLA: I like music and songs that celebrate the system.

FERDINAND: We have no music.

ISABELLA: If a minstrel dares to keep me sitting watching him for any length of time then I must be left with a warm, happy glow afterwards.

FERDINAND: That is our intention. Oh, I think I do love

the arts!

ISABELLA: I do not wish to be made to think. I do enough of that all day.

COLUMBUS: Absolutely.

ISABELLA: I want a simple story with sympathetic characters. I want the good to be rewarded and the bad to be punished.

COLUMBUS: Absolutely.

ISABELLA: You understand?

FERDINAND: Ludo has devised a little satire.

ISABELLA: We need art forms which appeal to everyone.

COLUMBUS: All things accessible! Absolutely!

ISABELLA: And which help disseminate our message. I want boys singing about girls and I want girls singing about how it's only love that matters!

COLUMBUS: We want songs about love!! We want songs about love!!

A silence.

They all stare at COLUMBUS.

FERDINAND: And who, might I ask, is this stooping lickspittle?

ISABELLA: This is Columbus.

FERDINAND: (*To COLUMBUS.*) You have changed. Where once you would swagger and strut, now you are all hunched up and shuffling.

COLUMBUS: My soul is in such torment, Majesty.

FERDINAND: You are like a shadow, man!

ISABELLA: Proceed, Ludo. Take me out of myself.

Relieve me of my troubles if only for an hour.

LUDO: If you would kindly dismount, Majesty.

FERDINAND: But of course.

FERDINAND dismounts. He slaps LUDO hard and approvingly on the back.

FERDINAND: Superlative steed, that!

ISABELLA coughs and splutters terribly.

Now, a little introduction. This piece is entitled *Columbus meets the Arawaks.*

COLUMBUS: I beg your pardon?

FERDINAND: And it is Ludo's own work. I take no credit apart from the occasional suggestion about timing.

ISABELLA: Let it begin then, God damn you, I have very little strength left.

FERDINAND: We hope that you will make allowances for us as it is our first foray into the realm of light entertainment.

ISABELLA: Let it begin, will you! Let it begin!

FERDINAND: (*Aside to LUDO.*) Remember what I said, boy. Make her laugh, make her convulse with merriment and you'll go free. Induce melancholy and profound thought, however, and you shall suffer for it. Lights!

Lights down.

LUDO now begins his mime/dumbshow. It is a bizarre and exaggerated retelling of Columbus' earlier narrative. LUDO is rather a skilled clown.

The audience watch in silence.

After a while, evidently piqued:

COLUMBUS: Your Majesty, I really must object!

ISABELLA holds up a hand to silence him. The show continues.

FERDINAND is looking hopefully at his wife who remains stony-faced.

After a while, COLUMBUS leads FERDINAND aside.

Your Majesty, might I have a word?

FERDINAND: What is it?

COLUMBUS: I have to admit to being rather displeased with this specific rendition of events.

FERDINAND: So am I. I thought she would find it funny.

COLUMBUS: It is a calumny.

FERDINAND: I am not responsible.

COLUMBUS: I ask that you command your savage to desist this instant.

FERDINAND: If she does not laugh at this 'Slaughter of the Children' section...

COLUMBUS: But...I am a national hero and I am being mocked, humiliated by a mere nig...

FERDINAND: Wait!

They watch as LUDO's strange performance continues. ISABELLA's brow is still furrowed.

COLUMBUS: (*Exiting.*) This is calumny! Calumny!

FERDINAND: Ssshh!!

They watch as LUDO's Columbus commits terrible crimes.

Suddenly ISABELLA lets out a huge, booming guffaw.

(*Punching the air.*) I think we have her!

ISABELLA: (*Laughing.*) Very good.

FERDINAND: (*Moving back to the bed.*) You approve?

ISABELLA: Oh, it's quite... (*She booms with laughter again.*) Oh, very good! Very good!

ISABELLA and FERDINAND laugh.

ISABELLA begins to throw coins to LUDO, laughing all the while, as he performs.

He catches them or scrambles around on the floor, desperately gathering them up.

The mime seems to end and the performance they are now laughing at is now the humiliation of the clown and the coins.

ISABELLA: (*Wiping the tears from her eyes.*) Ludo...that was quite wonderful. For those few minutes I was quite blissfully separated from the world. (*Suddenly altered.*) Yet now I feel my depression returning. I am the same as I was before. Ferdinand, quickly... take this down.

FERDINAND: (*With pen and paper.*) Yes?

ISABELLA: In order to...to preserve and strengthen our...our glorious system one must always seek to unite the people...against a common...a common enemy. Otherwise they may unite against us. And bring us down. Manipulate therefore their instinct for patriotism by controlling the means of information and generating their latent fears. It will often be necessary to invent enemies and external threats when they do not in actual fact insist. Foreign wars will always be vital for maintaining domestic stability, even as they open up foreign markets to our goods. Remember that, Ferdinand. Keep...them all...keep the whole world... scared. (*She coughs and wheezes terribly.*) And one more thing...

FERDINAND: Yes?

130

ISABELLA: Give...the Indians... Give the Indians...

FERDINAND: Yes, what, my darling? Give the Indians what?

ISABELLA: Give...the...Indians...back...their...land.

FERDINAND: It is too late, my darling. The whole process... We have begun something which now I doubt we can... Oh no, please God, no!

ISABELLA is dead.

FERDINAND throws himself on the bed, howling in despair.

LUDO: (*Aside.*) This whole performance simply emphasises, does it not, the sheer redundancy of satire in an age such as this.

Scene 8

ANGELINA at a desk, imperious, in command. GRUNT enters.

ANGELINA: So, Mr Grunt?

GRUNT: At your service, Madam.

ANGELINA: You have, it would appear, come a long way since you worked for my mistress.

GRUNT: I was told you had a...lucrative proposition for me?

ANGELINA: You are well informed.

GRUNT: And lucrative propositions...

ANGELINA: ...are the types of proposition upon which you thrive?

GRUNT: That is correct, Madam.

ANGELINA: Here. (*She hands him a large bag of gold.*) You will take ten per cent now. The balance payable on execution of the assignment.

GRUNT: (*Fondling the coins.*) This is... Fuck me!

ANGELINA: A lot of money?

GRUNT: A lot of money. Fuck me. That is correct, Madam.

ANGELINA: It seems that you are rising up your own particular ladder by killing. Is that right?

GRUNT: That is correct, Madam.

ANGELINA: Somebody wants somebody else murdered and they come to you. Is that right?

GRUNT: That is correct, Madam.

ANGELINA: And this line of work affords you job satisfaction, does it?

GRUNT: Despite one or two hairy moments, that is correct, Madam.

ANGELINA: And it evidently pays well?

GRUNT: That is correct, Madam. The wife gets whatever she wants and I get whatever I want. If you follow.

ANGELINA: And your children?

GRUNT: Private schooling.

ANGELINA: I understand.

GRUNT: The best.

ANGELINA: And that of course is your right.

GRUNT: Which was, as you can imagine, out of the question when I laboured as a mere toilet attendant.

ANGELINA: You have done well.

GRUNT: That is correct, Madam. The girl's coming on

nicely. Speaks well. Lots of hobbies, devout, kind-hearted and the boy is becoming proficient at music.

ANGELINA: So…the money interests you?

GRUNT: That is correct, Madam. This is more money than one man could ever need in an entire lifetime. There's enough coin here in this little sock for me to give up work, move back to England, buy meself a nice castle overlooking the sea, get meself a whole field of horses, an army of servants and spend the rest of me days scratching me belly or chasing me pleasures.

ANGELINA: Tell me, Mr Grunt…are you a royalist?

GRUNT: I care nothing either way.

ANGELINA: But their brutality?

GRUNT: They're not brutal to me. They kill well beyond my window. Though I do think the king's a bit of a cunt.

ANGELINA: But you will accept?

GRUNT: For this money there is very little I wouldn't do.

ANGELINA: Then listen closely…I want you to return to Spain and I want you to kill the King and the Queen.

A silence.

But be sure to kill them slowly. You must be able to describe their suffering to me on your return. I want you to bring back their tongues or their lips or their hearts or their livers and then you will receive the balance.

GRUNT: But the Queen…she is already dying.

ANGELINA: Then you must go quickly.

A silence as GRUNT deliberates.

GRUNT: This I…cannot do.

ANGELINA: You cannot?

GRUNT: That is...correct, Madam.

ANGELINA: (*Approaching.*) There is uncertainty in your eyes, Mr Grunt.

GRUNT: That is...incorrect, Madam.

ANGELINA: You cannot return my stare.

GRUNT: That is incorrect, Madam.

ANGELINA: Do I detect a blush, Mr Grunt?

GRUNT: That is incorrect, Madam.

ANGELINA: A smattering of crimson makes itself seen, this anarchic reddening suddenly comes to the surface of your skin beneath all the dirt and the stubble.

GRUNT: That is incorrect, Madam.

ANGELINA: How beyond the control of the white man is his blush? How it is one of the few things which shrugs off his policing.

GRUNT: I did not blush. That is incorrect, Madam.

ANGELINA: (*Up close.*) Your breath quickens.

GRUNT: Incorrect, Madam.

ANGELINA: I can hear your heart hammering the bars of its bony prison.

GRUNT: Incorrect, Madam.

ANGELINA: A bead of sweat moves through the deep and leathery creases of your forehead.

GRUNT: Incorrect, Madam.

ANGELINA: (*Putting a hand on his groin.*) And as for...

GRUNT: That is quite...incorrect, Madam.

She slowly kneels down before him, back to us.

Incorrect, Madam. That.

She goes down on him.

(*During this.*) As I say Madam…this is most irregular. Not part of the procedure, Madam. Not part of the procedure at all. As I say. As I say. As I say.

ANGELINA: (*Breaking off.*) You will accept?

Another silence.

GRUNT: That is correct, Madam.

She continues.

Scene 9

PHILIP and JUANA are seated at a table. In an awkward silence. PHILIP smiles at JUANA nervously. He coughs. She remains silent, sullen.

PHILIP: (*Nervously.*) We go to war again shortly.

No response from JUANA.

Insurrection everywhere.

No response from JUANA.

Tough measures are required.

No response from JUANA.

Unfortunate but what do you do?

No response from JUANA.

Question of economics, you see.

No response from JUANA.

They tell me our boy…the little emperor…he butted his

wet nurse this morning.

JUANA looks up.

Bust her gums and cracked two teeth, I'm told.

JUANA stares at him.

(*Nervous laugh.*) So that's a good sign then.

A silence.

After supper…after supper I'm afraid I have a meeting. With the man from the navy.

ANGELINA comes on with two covered dishes.

(*Rubbing his hands.*) Ah, splendid, splendid!

ANGELINA sets the dishes down in front of them.

My favourite time of the day, this!

JUANA: For what we are about to receive may the Lord make us truly thankful.

ALL: Amen.

ANGELINA uncovers the dishes.

The song of a muezzin hovers above.

Smells quite…wonderful.

JUANA and PHILIP begin to eat.

ANGELINA stands in the centre, choking back silent tears.

The song.

Scene 10

LUDO is whipping a semi-naked FERDINAND, a direct inversion of the opening scene. After a while FERDINAND holds up his hand. LUDO stops.

FERDINAND: (*Through the pain.*) So, you were saying... pleasure and pain spring from the same source?

LUDO: We cling to one and flee from the other.

FERDINAND: This is such a release, I confess.

LUDO: But are not the clinging and the fleeing exactly the same motion?

FERDINAND: You are right. Continue.

LUDO continues the whipping.

LUDO: And this motion, either towards pleasure or away from pain, is an assertion of the will and thus it strengthens...

FERDINAND: The ego, the self, Ludo!

LUDO: Precisely.

FERDINAND: And a self thus walled in brings with it only misery, isolation and suffering.

LUDO: You are beginning to understand, sire!

FERDINAND: I am so blessed to have you.

LUDO continues the whipping.

Harder, if you please.

LUDO whips him harder.

And then afterwards perhaps...a little more comedy? A little more...entertainment.

LUDO: What you will, sire.

FERDINAND: I miss her, Ludo. I must kill the time.

LUDO: Yes.

FERDINAND: I am so forsaken.

LUDO: Yes.

FERDINAND: You know forsaken, do you?

LUDO: I know it well.

FERDINAND: Loneliness never ends, you know.

LUDO: You have at least the memory of your love. This surely keeps you warm on the darkest of your nights?

FERDINAND signals for LUDO to stop the whipping.

FERDINAND: (*After a pause.*) I am not sure that I did, you know. Love. All those years and I suspect it was not what one calls…love. I have been thinking about it a great deal. Oh, it has all been such a hopeless, hopeless waste. And I, of all people, had every opportunity to get it right. But the constant rage, Ludo, the fear in my bones it… Oh, it's all the fault of my fucking parents, you see!

The ghost of ISABELLA appears above.

ISABELLA: Do not blame your parents, Ferdinand. A man must be responsible for his own soul.

FERDINAND: But they were so…brutal.

LUDO: Sire?

ISABELLA: One can always break the chain.

FERDINAND: Isabella, please!!

ISABELLA: You must die unloved, Ferdinand.

FERDINAND: Please, no!

ISABELLA: Just as I had to.

FERDINAND: No! Never! I loved you with all my heart.

LUDO: Your Majesty? You are unwell?

FERDINAND: Ludo, strike me! Strike me!

LUDO continues the whipping.

I miss you, Isabella! How I miss you! We all do! The nation is in mourning.

ISABELLA: You are a silly man.

FERDINAND: Silly? I know. I am silly, stupid, ridiculous. Harder, man! Harder!

ISABELLA: We have sown the seeds for the future. The world will progress according to our model.

FERDINAND: Does God love you, Bella? Is he...what's the word...grateful?

ISABELLA: He is... He is...

FERDINAND: Yes, yes? He is what, my darling? He is what?

ISABELLA: He is rather... (*A long pause.*) ...late.

FERDINAND: Late?

ISABELLA: (*Fading from view.*) Late. Yes. He seems to be rather...rather...late.

FERDINAND: God is late, Ludo. God is late. And now I feel the tears coming again!

FERDINAND sobs as LUDO continues whipping him.

GRUNT, in disguise, comes on with a tray. He stops in his crouch when he notices LUDO.

GRUNT: (*To himself.*) Ah, fuck it!

FERDINAND: Can we help you at all?

GRUNT: Medicine for Her Majesty.

FERDINAND draws his sword and approaches GRUNT.

FERDINAND: What did you say?

GRUNT: I said…

FERDINAND: You dare to mock my agony?

GRUNT: Something for her fever, Majesty.

FERDINAND: You, sir, are a little late with your fever cures!!

He attacks GRUNT who flings off his cloak and fights. It is vicious and violent.

Despite his years FERDINAND fights with ferocity.

GRUNT: (*To LUDO.*) Help me! Help me! This man is an animal! We are on the same side! You and me! Let's come together! Our lives can be beautiful! Beautiful!

FERDINAND makes a huge lunge at GRUNT and loses his sword in the process.

GRUNT flips him on his back and sits on his chest, sword poised over the King's head.

FERDINAND: Ludo! Ludo! Save me! Save me!

GRUNT: Say your prayers, Majesty.

FERDINAND: (*Calling off.*) Regicide! Regicide!

GRUNT: (*Laughing.*) A life of plenty is just one neckwound away!

FERDINAND: Ludo!

GRUNT: The revenge of the toilet attendant, Majesty!

GRUNT is about to bring down his sword.

As he does so LUDO grabs his arm and prevents the blow.

He twists GRUNT's arm and the sword drops.

Ah, fuck it!

LUDO holds his dagger to GRUNT's throat. He looks to the prostrate FERDINAND.

FERDINAND: Yes, yes, kill him, Ludo! Kill him! Kill him! Definitely kill him!

GRUNT: But I got little ones now!

LUDO: I'm sorry but these days I have become something of...something of...an employee.

LUDO swiftly slices GRUNT's throat.

GRUNT drops onto FERDINAND.

FERDINAND: (*From under GRUNT.*) You saved me, Ludo. You single-handedly saved the whole Empire.

LUDO: (*After a pause.*) Yes.

FERDINAND: I shall reward you.

LUDO: It was nothing.

FERDINAND: But first, Ludo...if you could kindly lift this man from the King. He bleeds all over him. Indeed he bleeds over him quite profusely.

LUDO lifts GRUNT off FERDINAND and drags him away.

FERDINAND rises to his feet. Naked from the waist up, he is a mass of whip wounds and is completely covered in GRUNT's blood. He spots his crown on the floor. He picks it up and replaces it on his head. As he does so regal music as before.

141

Scene 11

A dark street. The cries of seagulls and traders. JUANA in a cloak.

JUANA: I do not care for Antwerp. It reeks of mackerel.
And the seabirds are not the same as those which fly
over Spanish ports. These are nasty brutes, who scream
injustice at you as they pick the eyes from the rotting
heads of sheep. How they must envy their cousins in
Barcelona, Valencia, in Bilbao and Santander. Those are
altogether more benign, more at peace... What have we
eaten tonight? What have I drunk? I feel light-headed, I
feel as if the whole world were breaking apart beneath
my feet, I...

The full moon sheds a pale light on the scene.

And now the full ugliness and horror of modern night
life made plain, is made plain by the light of the moon.
God, the black teeth, the goggle eyes, the cheekscabs.
By the light of the moon...the moon... Do not stare
like that, please! Thank you! Oh these thoughts, these
thoughts... No, Alfonso, no...I will not be deflected
from my search for the truth.

Singing from a nearby pub. Shouting.

Oh, Spain, oh Spain. Why did they send me away
from you? I need to die in the sun, not in this hideous
swamp of putrefying mankind... And how unfamiliar
it all is. I walk along rain-spattered cobbles, hearing
the gurgling cries of the traders, tentatively stepping
over the gutters that bubble with excrement and the
innards of butchered beasts. The delicate fragrance of
the city. These are my people. I am their princess, soon
to be their queen and yet my whole life I have spent in
towers. They may be better folk than me, more real and
more deserving but oh to breathe again air uncorrupted
by their rotten lungs, to swim once more in a silence
uninterrupted by their merry banter!

She exits.

PHILIP enters from the other side. He is holding a book aloft.

PHILIP: The *Treatise on the Truth of the Catholic Faith, against Unbelievers*. One of only two copies in the whole of the country, I am told! The prized possession of my bookish spouse. A priceless edition! And I, shallow and vacuous man that I am, will happily exchange all the wisdom collected in these pages for just one more hour in the smooth young arms of my dark and melancholy whore! Now then, do we have time for a quick tug in the dark? (*He moves as if being yanked by his groin.*) Be serious, please. Why go to the Hole in the Wall? Have we not suffered enough there in the past? Think of that Welsh girl there with the rump like blancmange and the bed infested with lice! (*He moves in another direction as if being yanked by his groin.*) Now, o Tackle, you are being more sensible. Young, svelte girls who shudder to the touch and cast their eyes down as if it were their very first time. Not these chuckling harridans who always seem to be laughing at you as you penetrate them. I like at least the pretence of virginity. And with Juana…never since our wedding night have we recaptured our… The damage to a woman is just so… But no, sir…tonight we dine at the most exclusive of tables. No…tonight… tonight…we have no need for slops. (*He exits. After a while he re-enters. Thinks. Smiles to himself.*) For some reason, some strange force of vitality is flooding through my being tonight. As if I have imbibed some narcotic, some divine narcotic, that stimulates the blood and sharpens the mind. I feel…invincible…invincible… (*He goes back the way he came.*)

Scene 12

ANGELINA is revealed above, diamond tiara in her hair and dressed like a queen, seated on a throne made of books. She is reading from a volume. Below a bed.

VOICE OF THOMAS AQUINAS: Certain ancient philosophers denied the government of the world, saying that all things happened by chance. But such an opinion can be refuted as impossible in two ways. First, by observation of things themselves: for we observe that in nature things happen always or nearly always for the best; which would not be the case unless some sort of providence directed nature towards good as an end; which is to govern. Wherefore the unfailing order we observe in things is a sign of their being governed; for instance, if we enter a well-ordered house we gather therefrom the intention of him that put it in order.

ANGELINA slowly puts the book down.

JUANA enters. She looks around her.

JUANA: Oh, the opulence! The opulence of this shack, this cellar which used to be fit only for the salting of cod.

ANGELINA: Welcome. Welcome to my well-ordered little house.

JUANA: My books...you have all my books!

ANGELINA: You do not own the ideas in them.

JUANA: But I own the pages upon which the ideas are written! But your clothes, the jewels! They belong to me!

ANGELINA: Not so.

JUANA: What have you done to me! I give you your freedom and this is how you repay me! You steal from the hand that so generously offered you back your life!

ANGELINA: It is merely what is called the redistribution...

JUANA: Do not talk to me of that! That is ludicrous, that is so…so…utterly, utterly schoolboy!

ANGELINA: You have come here to discover the truth?

JUANA: Ah, this bed…this bed. See the decorative oak panelling, the exquisite little birds so expertly carved into the wood. This is a cot of true status! Only Flincker carves like this and he is in demand all over Europe! How could you possibly…? Oh, why do I waste my precious hours comparing, comparing?

ANGELINA: Your face is lined with fear, my lady.

JUANA: (*Pacing.*) I shudder with fear, yes. My whole spirit is in a torture. The organism contorts, it writhes with discomfort. Each vile thought arises unbidden from my brain and then torments me, derides me. And every thought is fear. It is terror, it is guilt, it is this dreadful insecurity, this constant comparison and oh…how the air we breathe commands us to hate ourselves. And this detestation of the self we export across the globe. I look to the future I see only decay and death. To the past and only regret and waste. I am as if scaling the sheer face of a cliff. Below me is an endless fall into hell, above me only dark, threatening clouds. I must learn to look only at the place where my hands rest upon the rock. Oh, I am demented, I am deranged! Can there, Angelina, be real love when there is always this terrible fear?

ANGELINA: You have spent your life believing that the meaning of life is love.

JUANA: But of course it is, of course it is! What would you know?

ANGELINA: This has been your mistake.

JUANA: What would you know? You, a mere…

ANGELINA: Please, my lady, hide yourself under the bed.

JUANA: The bed! Do not be ridiculous. I will dirty my dress!

ANGELINA: The bed holds the truth.

JUANA: Never!

ANGELINA: Quickly, quickly!

JUANA goes under the bed.

ANGELINA returns to her throne.

And hold your tongue still!

PHILIP enters.

PHILIP: (*Holding up the book.*) Your Majesty, I have the *Treatise against the Unbelievers*! But why, may I ask, have you been so eager to own it?

ANGELINA: It was composed to be used against the Jews and the Moors in Spain and to justify their subsequent annihilation.

PHILIP: This is a throne then made from the theories of Thomas Aquinas?

ANGELINA: It is estimated he wrote over eight million words.

PHILIP: The throne is large certainly!

ANGELINA: I have read enough.

PHILIP: And I have waited enough.

PHILIP climbs to where she is. He hands her the book.

She places it as part of her throne.

He kneels to her, his arms around her waist. She holds his head to her groin.

Ah, that beautiful black stench of you, Majesty! Let me

swim in your secret caverns.

ANGELINA: Not yet.

PHILIP: Not yet! But you have the book now! Because
of my addiction to your flesh my wife and I are almost
bankrupt! Do not tempt me! I shall force you! I shall be
forced to force you! I will not be responsible!

JUANA lets out a sob beneath the bed.

What was that?

ANGELINA: A woman sobbing.

PHILIP: Ah, one more little cry in the night, is it? One
more mother weeping over a dying child perhaps, or
some soldier who will now not be returning from the
wars? I cannot endure all this suffering around me, it is
so squalid, so thoroughly... uncivilised.

ANGELINA: Misery is not noble.

PHILIP: No! Never!

ANGELINA: It is sordid, unclean.

PHILIP: And rots the beauty from the heart of life. It is to
be avoided.

ANGELINA: But pleasure...?

PHILIP: On the other hand...

*PHILIP pulls ANGELINA off her throne and they drop
onto the bed. He pins her down and passionately makes love
to her. After a time:*

ANGELINA: Wait...I must blow out the candle.

PHILIP: No, please...I am almost done!

ANGELINA: One moment, my prince.

ANGELINA gets off the bed. She blows out a candle.

Darkness.

PHILIP: Come back to me, my beautiful girl. Oh, Angelina…I have to tell you. I am in love with you. You are, I am certain, the one great love of my life.

ANGELINA: But your wife?

PHILIP: Oh, don't talk to me of her, I beg you. She is like some huge whining lump of tedium which I am forced to deal with every day of my existence. Like some disgruntled hog she squats on my days and my nights. Come back to me, come back!

JUANA comes from beneath the bed. She takes ANGELINA's place in the clinch. It resumes.

ANGELINA relights the candle.

PHILIP continues oblivious.

ANGELINA looks at her beneath him and begins to laugh.

JUANA: (*Tearful.*) Please. Don't laugh. I beg you. Everyone. Is always. Laughing. Don't laugh at me. No. I am to be treated with respect. As a princess of the Empire. As a woman of learning. As a daughter of God. I was born to a high station. Born to achieve. So don't laugh. Please don't laugh. I am so anxious really. So full of anxiety and… anxiety and… and… and…

JUANA suddenly takes the chain of worry beads from around her neck.

PHILIP now climaxes. He looks down and sees JUANA beneath him. A long silence.

PHILIP: Beloved?

JUANA, with extreme savagery, wraps the beads around PHILIP's neck. She begins throttling him.

ANGELINA's laughter builds and distorts into something demonic.

The lights fade but the laughter continues in the darkness.

Lights up on ISABELLA, kneeling in prayer, sobbing with humility and remorse.

Lights up on FERDINAND being whipped once more by LUDO, who now wears his crown.

Lights up on ALFONSO above, nailed to his cross. He is in a torment of agony.

Lights up on ANGELINA seated on her throne of books. The laughter fades.

Then the sound of a modern dinner/cocktail party in full swing. Lights up on JUANA and PHILIP standing, glasses raised, addressing the audience.

PHILIP: We are the State, my friends.

JUANA: (*Through her tears.*) The State.

PHILIP: The Christian State.

JUANA: (*Through her tears.*) The Christian State.

PHILIP: We know what's right.

JUANA: (*Through her tears.*) For us and for everyone.

BOTH: So therefore we must impose our will upon the world.

ANGELINA sets fire to her throne. A golden glow and she smiles as she burns. The sound of the party builds.

Blackout.

The End.

Printed in the USA
CPSIA information can be obtained
at www.ICGtesting.com
LVHW020841171024
794056LV00002B/329